Ramesses the Great

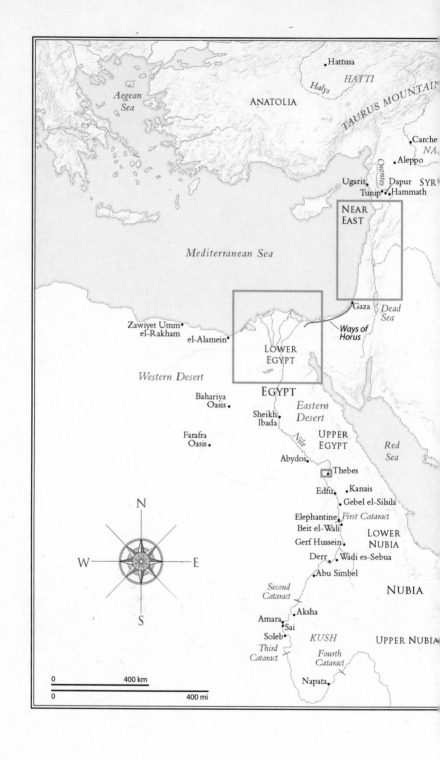

THE WORLD OF RAMESSES II

NEAR EAST

ASSYRIA

ZAGROS MOUNTAINS

Tigris

Babylon

BABYLONIA

Euphrates

Simyra
Eleutheros
Kadesh

Mediterranean Sea

AMURRU

Beqaa Valley

Byblos
Nahr el-Kelb
Beirut

UPE

Sidon
Adlun
Tyre

Damascus

GALILEE

al-Turra

Plain of Esdraelon
Beth Shan

Jordan Valley

CANAAN

PALESTINE

Dead Sea

MOAB

LOWER EGYPT

Mediterranean Sea

Tell el-Fara'in

Tell Abyad

Tell Abqa'in
Gharbaniyat
Kom el-Hisn

Per-Ramesses
Avaris

Heliopolis

Abusir
Saqqara
Giza
Memphis

Nile

Gurob

THEBES

Valley of the Kings

Qurna

Deir el-Medina

Ramesseum

Karnak

Valley of the Queens

Nile River

Luxor Temple

Ramesses the Great

Egypt's King of Kings

Toby Wilkinson

· ANCIENT LIVES ·

Yale

UNIVERSITY PRESS

NEW HAVEN & LONDON

Published with support from the Fund established in memory of
Oliver Baty Cunningham, a distinguished graduate of the Class of 1917, Yale College,
Captain, 15th United States Field Artillery, born in Chicago September 17, 1894,
and killed while on active duty near Thiaucourt, France, September 17, 1918,
the twenty-fourth anniversary of his birth.

Published with assistance from the foundation established
in memory of William McKean Brown.

Frontispiece: Beehive Mapping.
Map of the Battle of Kadesh by John Gilkes.

Yale University Press books may be purchased in quantity for
educational, business, or promotional use. For information, please e-mail
sales.press@yale.edu (U.S. office) or sales@yaleup.co.uk (U.K. office).

Set in the Yale typeface designed by Matthew Carter, and Louize,
designed by Matthieu Cortat, by Integrated Publishing Solutions.
Printed in Great Britain by TJ Books Limited, Padstow, Cornwall

Library of Congress Control Number: 2022941449
ISBN 978-0-300-25665-9 (hardcover : alk. paper)

A catalogue record for this book is available from the British Library.

10 9 8 7 6 5 4 3 2 1

MIX
Paper from
responsible sources
FSC
www.fsc.org   FSC® C013056

· ANCIENT LIVES ·

Ancient Lives unfolds the stories of thinkers, writers, kings, queens, conquerors, and politicians from all parts of the ancient world. Readers will come to know these figures in fully human dimensions, complete with foibles and flaws, and will see that the issues they faced — political conflicts, constraints based in gender or race, tensions between the private and public self — have changed very little over the course of millennia.

James Romm
Series Editor

Contents

Ramesses the Great

Introduction

Of the hundreds of kings who ruled ancient Egypt over the twenty-six centuries between its foundation as a nation-state (c. 2950 B.C.) and its absorption into the Hellenistic world (332 B.C.), only one is accorded the epithet "the Great" by modern Egyptologists. Ramesses II, known to his contemporaries as Usermaatra and to later legend as Ozymandias, bestrode the Nile Valley, and the wider ancient Near East, like a colossus. Indeed, he left more monuments — usually adorned with immense statues of himself — than any other pharaoh. He also sired more children, his sons and daughters numbering at least one hundred. His unusually long reign of sixty-six years and two months (1279–1213 B.C.) saw foes come and go, and three designated successors predecease their seemingly immortal father.[1]

These are the bare facts of an exceptional life, yet they do not in themselves explain the particular prominence of Ramesses' reputation, both in his own time and in every era since. Other pharaohs ruled over a larger empire, were more successful military leaders, achieved greater sophistication in art and architecture. As one nineteenth-century admirer of Ramesses had to admit, "It is safe to conclude that he was neither better nor worse than the general run of Oriental despots—that he was ruthless in war, prodigal in peace, rapacious of booty, and unsparing in the exercise of almost boundless power. Such pride and such despotism were, however, in strict accordance with immemorial precedent, and with the temper of the age in which he lived."[2] Ramesses, then, was not as exceptional as he might have wished to be. All kings of ancient Egypt surrounded themselves with pomp and pageantry, veiled themselves in a cloak of divinity, and took great pains to project their name and status, both to shore up their current position and to secure their eternal reputation. What was it about Ramesses II that made him different, special, and noteworthy in the long line of pharaohs? That is the overarching question I seek to address in this book.

In an examination of the life and times of Ramesses the Great, several factors come to the fore. First was the age in which he lived. The period known to Egyptologists as the New Kingdom (1539–1069 B.C.) marked the peak of ancient Egypt's power and prosperity. At the start of the New Kingdom, Egypt's rulers threw off foreign occupation and, to ensure there could be no repeat, carved out an empire of their own in the Levant and Nubia. At its greatest extent, Egyptian-controlled territory stretched from central Syria in the north to the Fourth Nile Cataract in the south, a distance of over a thousand miles. As an imperial power, Egypt enjoyed unfettered access to the gold mines of Nubia, the trading networks of the Near East, and the ports of the eastern Mediterranean. By the time Ramesses acceded to the throne, the era of empire building had ended but the era of imperial grandeur was at its zenith. Under Ramesses, Egypt was richer and more powerful than it had ever been before, or would ever be again. As a consequence, he had access to greater resources than any of his predecessors or successors.

Second, Ramesses used his position as a "great king" (one of an exclusive club of Bronze Age rulers which also included the rulers of the Hittites, Babylonia, and Assyria) to project Egypt's influence and secure its — and his — continued prominence. Although Ramesses came from a family of army generals and his dynasty was steeped in martial tradition, it was as a diplomatic strategist, not a military tactician, that he achieved his greatest successes. His armed campaigns generally ended in pyrrhic victories or stalemates, but they nevertheless served to maintain the status quo, giving Ramesses time to maneuver Egypt into a strong bargaining position. Previous rulers of the New Kingdom had been either invincible warriors or consummate diplomats; Ramesses was neither, but he was perhaps the first to employ both approaches in combination to navigate the shifting sands of Near Eastern politics to Egypt's advantage.

In addition, Ramesses acted on a scale that few other pharaohs, before or after, could match. His monuments were more impressive, even if many of them were reused from earlier epochs. His immediate dynasty was more numerous, even if many of his children died young. (But such was the fate of most people in ancient Egypt.) Ramesses' roles as builder and father were the most prominent means by which he sought to establish his monarchical and dynastic credentials.

Finally, in every facet of his reign, Ramesses seems to have been obsessed with his legitimacy and his legacy. This had much to do with the circumstances under which Ramesses' royal line, termed by Egyptologists the nineteenth dynasty (1292–1190 B.C.), had come to power. His grandfather, after whom he was named, had started life as a commoner, and Ramesses was acutely conscious of his family's plebeian origins. One of his abiding preoccupations was therefore to assert his legitimacy by reference to the unbroken sequence of Egypt's kings that stretched back to the dawn of history. At the same time, Ramesses wanted to be seen as the progenitor of his own dynasty and the founder of a new order. Hence, the character of his reign presents a complex amalgam of tradition and innovation. The result was a period of uncommonly rich cultural invention and expression.

When it came to usurping the statues of earlier rulers—something Ramesses did with great enthusiasm—his strong preference was for the works of the twelfth and eighteenth dynasties, not just because they were especially well crafted, and especially large, but also because they epitomized the classical eras of the past and hence symbolized continuity. At the same time, Ramesses' artists absorbed elements from the revolutionary style of an earlier reign (that of Akhenaten, "the heretic pharaoh," who died just fifty-seven years before Ramesses' accession), deploying the same naturalism and emotional sensitivity, albeit in a more traditional style. Under Ramesses' patronage, the large-scale depiction of battle scenes—perhaps his favorite artistic genre—broke free of the earlier system of rigid registers to flow across entire walls. In the field of literature, too, the shackles of tradition were thrown off, as new texts were composed for the first time in the modern spoken vernacular—even as the royal court and scribal training schools were showing a renewed interest in the classical writers of the past. And in religious matters, perhaps the most tradition-bound sphere of ancient Egyptian culture, the choice of texts for the decoration of Ramesses' royal tomb demonstrated a fresh new direction.[3]

Despite such cultural innovation, however, Ramesses is best known today not for the sophistication of his court but for his unsurpassed ambition and self-promotion. His posthumous reputation was no accident; it arose out of a propaganda campaign that was as relentlessly pursued as it was carefully crafted. As a result, he still looms large, in every sense, in the modern Western imagination. Yet Ramesses himself remains something of an enigma. Despite the survival of a large range of textual, artistic, and architectural evidence from his long reign (some of the texts no doubt composed to Ramesses' own instructions), it is almost impossible to write a conventional biography of a figure so far removed in space, time, and culture from today.[4] Ancient Egyptian kings do not lend themselves to examination as individuals, for there is simply none of the material upon which the biographer usually relies: no private correspondence, only diplomatic letters written in a formal, highly structured style; no firsthand accounts of a person, only formulaic paeans of praise to his royal status. In his own time, Ramesses was hedged about with divinity and cloaked in a veil of pomp, precedent, and propaganda. As a result, like Egypt's other pharaohs, he can appear to modern eyes as an exotic, quasi-mythical, almost superhuman figure.

While a detailed examination of Ramesses' personality lies out of reach (though some commentators have tried it), what is possible is to go beyond a mere enumeration of his achievements and delve more deeply into the particular times, circumstances, and relationships that lay behind them. By considering Ramesses' preoccupations and preferences as expressed in the surviving archaeological and textual record, we may perhaps infer something of his character and motives. In such a way, we may catch a glimpse of the man behind Shelley's "shattered visage" — a man who in his own time was revered as a god, and who in every era since has been acclaimed as "king of kings."

CHAPTER ONE

Great Expectations

In the late summer of 1322 B.C., the king of Egypt, Tutankhamun, died unexpectedly. He was still in his teens. His death seems to have come without warning – the tomb that was being prepared for him in the ancestral royal necropolis of Thebes was still far from finished – but it cannot have been wholly surprising. For Tutankhamun, whose father and mother were closely related, suffered from a series of congenital abnormalities, ranging from a cleft palate to a club foot, and had been frail since childhood, walking with the help of a stick. He had also suffered periodic bouts of malaria, which weakened his slender frame still further. His death at a young age was, in fact, the norm in ancient Egypt, where the average life expectancy hovered around the mid-thirties, and where reaching forty or fifty years was considered a rare achievement.

Tutankhamun's untimely demise must have been a personal tragedy for his young wife and half-sister, Ankhesenamun (who had also suffered a miscarriage and a still-birth some time earlier), but for Egypt it was a calamity. It marked the demise of a royal house that had occupied the throne for more than two centuries.

The eighteenth dynasty, as it is termed today, had presided over a golden age of pharaonic civilization: restoring Egyptian independence and pride after a period of foreign rule; carving out an empire in the Levant and Nubia; erecting the largest, most dazzling temples Egypt had ever seen; and transforming the ruling family's hometown of Thebes into a spectacular religious capital and one of the greatest cities of the ancient world. The rule of the eighteenth dynasty must have seemed destined to last forever. But Tutankhamun and his queen, with no surviving children of their own, were the last of their line. The crisis of succession sparked by the pharaoh's death threatened the stability of the whole country. In the absence of a male blood relative to claim the throne, only one institution was strong enough to fill the power vacuum and prevent what the Egyptians feared most, a descent into anarchy and chaos. That institution was the army.

One of the side effects of the empire building undertaken by Tutankhamun's forebears had been the creation of a permanent, professional military force. In earlier eras, Egypt had relied on conscripts and mercenaries, levying troops as and when the need arose. But for a newly established imperial power, with vassals and colonies strung out from Syria in the north to Upper Nubia in the south, such means were no longer sufficient. Safeguarding the allegiance of troublesome client states and maintaining Egyptian control of subject territory required the presence of garrison troops, backed up by regular shows of force to quell unrest and put down would-be insurrections. Only a standing army, with a professional command structure, could deliver such a capability.

The creation of a military class had been one of the most significant acts of the early eighteenth dynasty, and over the succeeding generations Egypt had been profoundly changed as a result. Military symbols and themes first crept into, then came to dominate, royal iconography. Weapons of war, notably chariots, became the most prized possessions of the ruling elite. And the army took its place alongside the priesthood as one of the major power blocs in society. A reorganization in the late eighteenth dynasty divided the military into two distinct corps, infantry and chariotry. While the infantry formed the backbone of the army, the chariotry provided the elite shock troops, used with devastating effect to harry a weakened opponent on the field of battle and turn a victory into a rout. Egypt also had a marine corps, with one major base in the northeastern Nile Delta (named, appropriately, Perunefer, "bon voyage") and another at the port of the capital city, Memphis. Indeed, troops were stationed not just on Egypt's borders and in its foreign territories but within the country itself. A large garrison of reservists stationed outside Memphis could be deployed rapidly in emergencies, and no doubt also served as a powerful deterrent against domestic insurrection. The army stood ready to protect Egypt from within as well as from without.

When Tutankhamun's father, Akhenaten, had overturned the established order, closing the major temples, abandoning Thebes and Memphis, and founding a new capital city in honor of his personal god, the orb of the visible sun (Aten), he had needed to appoint trusted confidants to his regime: men without ties to the old ways, men on whose loyalty he could count without hesitation. More often than not, he turned to the military. Two such figures achieved particular prominence at court. Both were of modest, provincial origins; both used their army connections to advance their careers. The elder by perhaps a few years was named Ay, and he served Akhenaten as commander of chariotry. His colleague, Horemheb, must have started his rise to power at the same time, but he subsequently drew a discreet veil over this stage of his career; his rise to public prominence occurred instead in the reign of Tutankhamun, when Horemheb emerged as commander-in-chief of the army and "general of generals."

Horemheb's status under Tutankhamun was not solely military; he also held high civilian office, serving as "king's deputy in the entire land." In effect, he ran the country on behalf of the boy pharaoh. Ay, who had probably retired from active service but was still very much the elder statesman, gloried in the title "god's father," signifying his closeness to the throne. Throughout most of Tutankhamun's nine-year reign, these two military men must have dominated the royal court, just as they guided the affairs of state. At the pharaoh's death, they were left holding the reins of power. Horemheb, as the king's appointed deputy, might have expected to succeed. But instead, it was Ay who claimed the throne. Whether Ay took advantage of Horemheb's temporary absence on campaign (the generalissimo was most likely in Syria, leading an ultimately unsuccessful attempt to recapture the rebel city of Kadesh), or whether the arrangement between the two men was amicable is uncertain. In any case, Ay did not enjoy a long reign. Already a man of advanced age (especially for ancient Egypt), he lived for only three or four years more, and was duly succeeded as pharaoh by Horemheb. As the throne passed from one incumbent to another, the army's grip on power never faltered.

Horemheb reigned as he had lived: his twenty-seven years on the throne were characterized by military efficiency and an ever-expanding role for the army in all aspects of Egyptian life. In restoring and reestablishing the temples and cults that had been closed by Akhenaten, Horemheb restaffed them with "lay-priests and lector-priests from the pick of the infantry." In promulgating a new series of laws, "to drive out chaos and destroy falsehood," he paid special attention to the order and discipline of the armed forces.[1] According to Horemheb's Edict, for example, any soldier found guilty of stealing a hide — even to supplement his basic kit — would be punished severely with a hundred blows and five open wounds, in addition to the confiscation of the stolen items. The measures also decreed enhanced rewards for members of the king's bodyguard, in tandem with a new protocol for the innermost chambers of the palace, to ensure that the king's personal security was as tight as possible. With his detailed knowledge of military tactics, the pharaoh was not going to take any chances with his own protection.

Perhaps the most significant decision of Horemheb's reign concerned neither the reinstatement of the old cults nor the restoration of law and order but the royal succession. In the absence of an heir of his own, he did what Tutankhamun had done in the same position: appointed an army officer as his "deputy and executive" and hence his designated successor. The military had already ensured a smooth transition of power on two occasions. Guaranteeing a third was only prudent.

This latest army commander to take his place as king-in-waiting was a man from the eastern Nile Delta by the name of Paramessu. He came from a respectable military family, his father, Seti, having served as a troop commander and possibly royal envoy in Palestine during the reign of Akhenaten.[2] Paramessu himself seems to have begun his career as a lowly stablemaster before being promoted to Master of the Horse (possibly under Tutankhamun or Ay), then troop commander, commander-in-chief of the army (in the reign of Horemheb), and finally vizier. In this last office, the highest in the civilian administration, Paramessu dedicated a statue of himself, in the age-old pose of a scribe, in the great temple of Amun-Ra at Karnak, the most prestigious religious institution in all Egypt.

Paramessu is likely to have entered the army at about the same time as Horemheb, and probably served alongside him. The two men were close in age, and clearly enjoyed a bond of trust. What marked out Paramessu as the ideal choice for heir apparent, however, was not only his military background but also his family circumstances. Paramessu was married to a woman named Satra, and whereas Horemheb and his wife were without an heir, Paramessu and Satra had a son — and a grandson. The son, Seti (named for his grandfather), had been born about the time of Horemheb's accession and was thus probably in his twenties when his father was appointed heir apparent. Seti was married, as his family background would have all but demanded, to the daughter of a chariotry officer; her name was Tuya. The young couple had already started a family. Their first son, who died in infancy, was followed by a daughter, Tia, then a second son, named Ramesses. Hence, by the time Paramessu was chosen as heir to the throne, he, Seti, and the baby Ramesses together formed a ready-made dynasty.[3] Horemheb could therefore live out his last days secure in the knowledge that the kingship would be in safe army hands for generations to come.

Even before being appointed vizier and next in line, Paramessu would have received a rigorous training in Horemheb's preferred approach to law and order. Vivid details of life in the armed forces during Horemheb's tenure as commander-in-chief are recorded on the walls of his tomb chapel at Saqqara, a monument built to celebrate his achievements as a private citizen before he became king. Among the unnamed officers who are shown accompanying Horemheb in the performance of his official duties, one may be Paramessu. If so, he would have witnessed at first hand Horemheb's modus operandi. In Horemheb's military camp, messenger boys carried instructions on the double from tent to tent, while the general himself received pleas for clemency from foreign emissaries, who prostrated themselves "seven times on the belly and seven times on the back."[4] Prisoners of war from campaigns in the Levant and Nubia lined up before the commander to await their fate. The Syrian prisoners, with wooden manacles on their wrists and ropes around their necks, were paraded, pushed, and cajoled by Egyptian soldiers. The Kushite chief prostrated himself before the general while Egyptian soldiers assaulted his men, beating them with sticks and punching them on the jaw. Looking on impassively, army scribes recorded every detail. In the prosecution of war, as in the affairs of peace, Horemheb's approach was uncompromising.

By the time Horemheb died, around 1292 B.C., Paramessu was well prepared for the highest office in the land. He had had ample time to think about his priorities and how he wished to define his reign—the first of a new ruling family (known to Egyptologists as the nineteenth dynasty).[5] The new pharaoh's first act on succeeding to the throne was to announce his official titulary. Names and titles, especially those belonging to the king, carried enormous symbolic weight in ancient Egypt. Foremost among the many royal titles borne by an Egyptian pharaoh was his throne name, the moniker by which he would be known in all official documents. The exact formulation of a throne name—which was composed from a small number of standard elements brought together in combination to form a terse, theological statement—effectively set the tone for the new reign. (The formulation of the Japanese emperor's throne name continues the same tradition today.) Conscious of his status as founder of a new royal line, Paramessu deliberately modeled his throne name on that borne by the founder of the eighteenth dynasty, Ahmose. Where Ahmose had been known as Nebpehtyra (Neb-pehty-ra: "Ra is lord of strength"), Paramessu chose Menpehtyra (Men-pehty-ra: "Ra is enduring in strength"). Both names had strong military overtones. Indeed, Ahmose had ushered in Egypt's imperial age through a series of foreign campaigns which had also laid the foundations for the creation of a professional army.

At the same time that he adopted a throne name redolent of history and dynastic promise, Paramessu chose to recast his birth name to suit his new regal identity. Paramessu, meaning "the sun [god] has created him," was a good enough Egyptian name, but the vernacular inclusion of the definite article "Pa" before the name of the god betrayed Paramessu's commoner background. This was the language spoken in ordinary Egyptian households, not at court. Royal protocol demanded the use of the traditional, classical language, frozen in time by centuries of precedent. Hence, in a swift, small, but immensely significant change, Paramessu, from the moment of his accession, became Ramessu (more commonly rendered by Egyptologists as Ramesses). The meaning stayed the same, but the language was now unimpeachably pharaonic.

Ramesses I's initial act as king would have been to officiate at his predecessor's burial, for Egyptian tradition held that the person carrying out the funeral obsequies gained legitimacy as the heir of the deceased. No sooner had the tomb of Horemheb been sealed than Ramesses began a sepulcher of his own, directly opposite that of his predecessor and patron. From the outset, the tomb of Ramesses I was designed at a much smaller scale than previous royal burials: an indication, perhaps, that Ramesses — by now in his fifties — knew that his time on the throne was likely to be limited. Better a small completed tomb than a large incomplete one. In other projects, he dedicated temples in Nubia and Palestine, thus symbolically emphasizing Egyptian control over its subject territories. He also launched a successful military foray into Canaan (the southernmost province of Egyptian-controlled western Asia), to demonstrate his resolve — although the campaign was led by his son, Seti.

Ramesses I's most ambitious project by far was at Karnak, where he began work on a new monumental gateway (which Egyptologists call a pylon), and the transformation of Horemheb's open court into a grand hypostyle hall. The intention seems to have been to equal, if not surpass, the temple-building activities of the great kings of the past. Thanks to the largesse of successive eighteenth-dynasty rulers, the temple of Amun-Ra had been transformed over the generations into the richest, most powerful, and most significant religious foundation in the country. By enhancing and adorning it, Ramesses no doubt hoped to secure divine and theological favor for himself and his nascent dynasty. Moreover, a very visible project in the spiritual heartland of Thebes would have been highly symbolic for a man whose family came from the opposite end of the country, and whose personal religious attachments (as indicated by the names of his male descendants) swung more toward the northern gods, Seth of Avaris and Ra of Heliopolis.

Despite its bold objectives, Ramesses I's project at Karnak had barely started when its royal sponsor died. He had reigned for fewer than two years. He had prepared for this moment, however, appointing Seti vizier, then co-regent, to ensure a smooth succession. It would fall to Ramesses' son and young grandson to continue his work, realize his vision, and secure his dynasty.

ROYAL APPRENTICE

Seti, now in his mid-thirties, with his son Ramesses approaching his teens, acceded to the throne.[6] Like his father before him, he chose a throne name with powerful connotations. Where Ramesses I had recalled Ahmose, Seti I sought to channel not one but two of the greatest rulers of the eighteenth dynasty: the warrior-pharaoh Thutmose III (throne name Menkheperra) and the builder supreme Amenhotep III (Nebmaatra). Seti I's chosen throne name combined elements of both: Menmaatra. And the new king fully intended his deeds to match his words.

Within months of his accession, Seti I personally led a campaign to demonstrate Egyptian control over the Ways of Horus, the strategic land bridge between Egypt and the Levant that followed the north coast of the Sinai Peninsula. It was probably little more than a routine show of force: although the local Bedouin tribes had sown disorder, threatening stability, there is no indication that the Ways of Horus had been lost to Egyptian control. Nonetheless, Seti's "victorious" entry into Gaza, the administrative center of Egyptian-controlled Canaan, was celebrated with the usual pomp and ceremony. As the king and his three battle divisions moved north, however, reports reached him of a more serious challenge to Egyptian authority. A rebel leader had gathered a large force and succeeded in capturing the Egyptian garrison town of Beth Shan (present-day Beit She'an). Such a threat to pharaonic control could not be ignored. Seti swiftly dispatched his army to recapture Beth Shan, together with Hammath (the hometown of the rebel leader) and Yenoam (which guarded the approach from Galilee). "In the space of a day," as the official account later boasted, "they fell to the power of His Majesty."[7] This swift and decisive action had secured the strategically important Plain of Esdraelon, pacifying and reasserting Egyptian hegemony over a swath of subject territory the length of the Jordan Valley and all the way up the Mediterranean coast to the port of Tyre. The king erected a victory stela at Beth Shan before returning home in glory.

Subsequent campaigns over the next two or three years saw the Egyptian army return to Canaan, and to the more distant province of Upe, and establish control over the key ports of Sidon, Byblos

(Jubail), and Simyra (Tell Kazel). While pleasing successes, these were in reality little local victories against minor, troublesome city-states. The real enemy — and a much more formidable foe — was Egypt's rival for imperial dominance in the Near East, the Kingdom of the Hittites.[8]

During these military expeditions in the early part of his reign, Seti kept his son Ramesses safely at home in Egypt. But it was not long before the prince began his formal induction into the affairs of kingship. At about the age of ten, probably to coincide with his father's accession, he was recognized as "eldest son" (crown prince), and given titular control of the army. A later retrospective inscription, carved when Ramesses had become king, records obsequious courtiers lauding him in the following terms: "Every matter has come to your attention since you began to deputize in this land. You managed affairs when you were in the egg, in your office of child heir. The business of the Two Banks [Egypt] was told to you when you were a child with a sidelock. No pious deed came to pass without being under your guidance. No commission was initiated without you. You acted as commander of the army when you were a youth of ten years." In another inscription, carved inside Seti I's temple at Abydos, Ramesses himself claims: "It was Menmaatra who nurtured me, and the Lord of All himself who promoted me, when I was [still] a child, until I could establish my rule; for he had given me the land when I was in the egg. The officials kissed the ground before me when I was installed as eldest son and heir upon the throne of Geb, and when I reported [the affairs of] the Two Lands as commander of the infantry and chariotry."[9] If these inscriptions are to be taken at face value, Ramesses was entrusted even as a boy with a number of duties to prepare him for the throne, including supervising public works, and with a level of responsibility for the two branches of the army.

Nor was Ramesses' military appointment merely ceremonial. In his father's fourth or fifth year on the throne, when Ramesses was about fourteen, the prince gained his first taste of military action during a brief campaign to defend the western Delta approaches against incursion by Libyan tribes. The encounter, though small-scale, must have been a defining moment for the royal apprentice. Indeed, the western frontier would be the focus of major works when Ramesses became king.

Having been inducted into the ways of warfare, Ramesses participated in an altogether more serious campaign a year or two later. The focus this time was the Levant, the goal the subjugation of Amurru (the northernmost, most troublesome of Egypt's Near Eastern provinces) and the recapture of the strategic stronghold of Kadesh (Tell Nebi Mend), a fortified town on the River Orontes (Nahr el-Asi) in northern Syria. Both Amurru and Kadesh, which had first been seized for Egypt by the warrior kings of the eighteenth dynasty, had proven fickle allies. Their rulers were adept at playing off one great power against another. In the mid-eighteenth dynasty, they had vacillated between Egypt and the Kingdom of Mittani. Since the time of Tutankhamun, the Hittites had supplanted Mittani as Egypt's rival for dominance in the Near East. Horemheb, while still a general, had tried to subdue Kadesh once and for all, but it reverted to Hittite control soon after the Egyptian troops left. Now Seti I attempted the same. To his frustration, however, the Hittites declined to engage. He nonetheless portrayed this as a great victory, erecting a triumphal stela at Kadesh and recording the "battle" on the temple walls of Karnak. But the town, and the whole province of Amurru, again reverted to Hittite control when the Egyptians departed. As with the Libyan campaign, the Kadesh mission left an indelible mark on the young Ramesses. Recapturing the town would fester in his mind as unfinished business, and the attempt to complete his father's work would in time define his reign.

The pharaonic empire of the nineteenth dynasty comprised territory to the south of Egypt as well as to the north. Just as the provinces and city-states of Syria-Palestine could prove restive, so too could the subject lands of Nubia, known to the ancient Egyptians as Kush. In the eighth year of Seti's reign, Egypt launched a major offensive to secure its southern interests. The superior training and equipment of the Egyptian army gave it a huge advantage over its Kushite adversary. In the space of a single week, the pharaoh's forces marched through the southern oases of the Libyan Desert to attack Kush along its vulnerable western flank, crush the rebellion, and capture hundreds of prisoners of war. Ramesses seems to have taken no part in this campaign, but news of the Egyptian army's success must have left a strong impression on the young, ambitious prince; in due course, Nubia would be the focus for the most extravagant and commanding projection of royal power of his entire reign.

The first and foremost duty of an Egyptian king was to defend his country—and, by extension, the whole of creation—from the forces of disorder and chaos (epitomized, in pharaonic religion and iconography, by foreign enemies). Seti I certainly took this duty seriously, and he ensured that his son and heir was given opportunities to develop the martial prowess which had brought the nineteenth dynasty to power and by which it set such great store. But a pharaoh had another abiding duty: to honor and propitiate the gods by enhancing and beautifying their temples through lavish building works. Here, too, Seti consciously emulated the high standards set by the great kings of the eighteenth dynasty. Since the time of Ahmose, most of the major temples of Upper Egypt had been constructed not from the soft limestone found in the northern part of Egypt but from the hard-wearing sandstone which characterizes the geology of the southernmost Nile Valley. The principal quarry for sandstone, throughout the eighteenth and nineteenth dynasties, was at the site of Gebel el-Silsila.[10] Here the cliffs approach close to the river, making it easier to move vast, heavy blocks of stone to waiting barges and transport them to their final destinations. Even today the cliffs at Gebel el-Silsila bear the tool marks of the stonemasons who hewed countless tons of building material from the rose-colored rocks. Seti I was all too aware of the importance of the quarry, and its workers, for his construction projects; in the sixth year of his reign he made a point of publicly improving the rations of the quarrymen. Elsewhere in Upper Egypt there were further natural riches to be exploited, and Seti took a personal interest in the gold mines of the eastern desert, establishing a well and a rest station for the workers at the site of Kanais, halfway between the Nile and the mines themselves. By such means did an Egyptian king demonstrate his mastery over the forces of nature, as well as his concern for his people and his piety toward the gods.

All the while, Ramesses followed his father's actions and sought to emulate them as part of his own royal apprenticeship. Hence, while Seti's workmen were digging a well on the road to the gold mines, Ramesses was supervising quarrying missions of his own at the First Nile Cataract, source of the gray and pink granite so prized for royal statuary and architectural elements (notably obelisks, columns, lintels, and doorjambs). An inscription left by the mission at the granite quarries recorded that "His Majesty (life, prosperity, health!) ordered a multitude of works: creating huge obelisks and great and wonderful statues in the name of His Majesty (life, prosperity, health!). He built great barges for transporting them—with ships' crews to match—and ferrying them from the quarry, while high officials and transport engineers hurried [the work along]. And his eldest son was at their head, doing good deeds for His Majesty."[11]

Such practical experience meant that by the time Ramesses reached his late teens or early twenties, he was deemed ready to undertake more serious and strenuous commissions on behalf of his father. A minor revolt in Lower Nubia — troublesome Kush again — provided the perfect opportunity for Ramesses to demonstrate his credentials and take sole command of an Egyptian military force for the first time. The result, one suspects, was never in doubt: the inevitable crushing victory was marked with the construction of a small rock-cut temple at the site known today as Beit el-Wali, its walls decorated with scenes of weeping Nubians and vanquished foes offering tribute to their pharaonic overlord.[12] Erecting a temple to commemorate Egyptian hegemony over Nubia would prove a favorite tactic throughout Ramesses' career.

The reliefs at Beit el-Wali also show images of battle against Syrian and Libyan enemies, although these particular scenes may be symbolic rather than a record of actual events. But scattered textual references suggest some military campaigning in the west during Ramesses' reign, and he may well have taken part in — or at least claimed the credit for — a successful raid against pirates harrying the coastal fringe of the western Nile Delta. Certainly, prisoners of war captured during this maneuver, members of a feared and warlike band called the Sherden, were later employed as mercenaries in Ramesses' own army.[13] In the great battle scenes carved for Seti I at about the same time in the hypostyle hall at Karnak — a continuation of Ramesses I's unfinished project — the younger Ramesses had himself inserted into key scenes to show him fighting by his father's side, walking behind his father's chariot, or helping to kill a Libyan. (The figure of Ramesses was carved over that of a troop captain called Mehy. It was entirely in keeping with phara-onic tradition that honoring the heir to the throne should take precedence over recognizing the achievements of a mere com-moner, however valiant.) Taken together, the evidence indicates that in the later campaigns of Seti I's reign, Ramesses took an in-creasingly central role.

Seti's construction work at Karnak, designed to realize his fa-ther's ambition of creating a magnificent hypostyle hall at the front of the great temple, was not the only ambitious building project of his reign, nor the only one in which his son took a keen personal interest. Other major works included additions to the temple of Ptah at Memphis and the temple of Ra at Heliopolis. The nine-teenth dynasty's special reverence for these two northern cult cen-ters reflected its own northern origins, as did Seti's construction of a summer palace at Avaris in the northeastern Delta, the home-town of his dynasty. In time, Ramesses would stamp his own mark on all three sites.

But there was another site, far away from these northern cities, that held special resonance and reverence for Seti I and his el-dest son. Abydos, in Upper Egypt, was uniquely sacred to ancient Egyptians because of its status as the cult center of Osiris, lord of the dead and king of the underworld, and burial place of Egypt's earliest kings. Nowhere else in the Nile Valley was the aura of antique royalty and divine kingship as powerful as at Abydos. The nineteenth dynasty, for all its military might and swagger, was acutely conscious of its plebeian origins. Enhancements and benefactions to the principal state cults at Heliopolis, Memphis, and Karnak certainly helped to bolster the legitimacy of Seti I and his family, but Abydos was the place where the Egyptian monar-chy had begun, where the complex relationship between kingship and divinity was most powerfully celebrated. Seti's greatest building project, therefore, was focused on Abydos; within sight of the sanctuary of Osiris, and dominating the approach to the town from the river, it comprised nothing less than the creation of a dynastic temple to rival the temples of the gods.[14]

The ritual significance of Seti I's temple at Abydos can be judged not only from the spectacular painted reliefs on the interior walls (among the best preserved in Egypt, they retain their color and sheen, belying their three thousand years) but also from the architecture of the building itself. Where most Egyptian temples had but a single sanctuary, dedicated to the resident deity, Seti I's temple has seven. Pride of place, at the heart of the temple, is given to the triad of deities most closely associated with Abydos: Osiris, his sister-wife Isis, and their son Horus. The principal state gods of Egypt—Ra of Heliopolis, Ptah of Memphis, and Amun-Ra of Karnak—are honored in adjacent chapels. The seventh sanctuary is dedicated to the deified form of Seti himself, putting the king on a par with the supreme divine powers of the ancient Egyptian world and underworld. While the divinity of kingship was a central tenet of pharaonic religion from the very beginning of Egyptian history, it was unusual for a reigning king to be worshipped directly as a god during his lifetime. As in other aspects of his reign, Seti I seems to have taken his inspiration from Amenhotep III of the eighteenth dynasty.

At Abydos, Seti I also built a small memorial chapel for his father, Ramesses I. But the dynastic character of the main edifice is most clearly demonstrated in its distinctive feature, the hall of ancestors or Abydos king list. At the rear of the temple, far away from the public realm, one entire wall of a long corridor is decorated with a scene showing Seti I, with his eldest son and heir, Ramesses, by his side, making offerings to the names of his royal predecessors, all the way back to Menes, legendary first king of the first

Dynastic ambition: Prince Ramesses depicted in his father's temple at Abydos (author photo).

dynasty and unifier of Egypt. Egyptologists treasure the Abydos king list as a unique historical source, providing evidence for the ancient Egyptians' knowledge of their own past and an insight into which kings were considered legitimate (and fit to be included in the list) and which were not. But for Seti and Ramesses, the scene had a more practical purpose: by associating them with the monarchs of the past from the beginning of Egyptian history, the list emphasized the place of father and son in the unbroken line of pharaonic authority and proclaimed their incontestable legitimacy. Abydos was where the nineteenth dynasty declared and affirmed its right to rule.

By showing Prince Ramesses offering to his ancestors alongside his father, the Abydos king list not only projected monarchy back to the origins of history, it also projected it forward by anticipating the succession of the next pharaoh. On a more practical level, one of the mechanisms devised by ancient Egyptian rulers to guarantee a smooth transition from one reign to the next was the institution of co-regency, whereby the heir would be crowned in his father's lifetime. And it was at Abydos that Ramesses' own elevation, from eldest son and heir to co-regent with his father, was formally announced and recorded. In a lengthy inscription inside the temple, Ramesses recalled this decisive moment in his royal apprenticeship: "When my father appeared before the people, I a child in his arms, he said concerning me, 'Raise him up as king, that I may see his perfection while I am still alive.' He summoned the chamberlains to fix the regalia on my brow. 'Place the crown on his head'—so he said concerning me when he was still on earth. He established me with private apartments and beauties of the palace as royal attendants. He selected women for me." From this moment on, Ramesses ruled jointly with his father (although no separate regnal years were assigned to him).[15] The transition was also marked elsewhere in the hall of ancestors by the subtle addition of the new king's titles in a scene showing him and his father offering to the gods. For his throne name, Ramesses chose the formulation Usermaatra; it paid due homage to his father (Menmaatra) while introducing the new element *user* (powerful) into the royal titulary. It was a conscious statement that power and might would define the new reign.

The proclamation of the co-regency between Seti and Ramesses turned out to have been a prescient move. For within a few years at most (probably fewer than two), the father died in his late forties, leaving the son as sole pharaoh. The reign of Ramesses II had begun in earnest.

HIS FATHER'S SON

Ramesses was in his early twenties when he took on the mantle of pharaonic kingship, ruling alone over a vast territory stretching from Syria-Palestine in the north to the Fourth Nile Cataract in the south.[16] His royal training had been thorough, comprising both military and civilian duties, and his formal co-regency had prepared him for the throne. His first duty was to supervise the arrangements for the funeral and burial of his father. Seti I seems to have died in late May, in his summer palace at Avaris (Tell el-Dab'a); so after the seventy-day period of mummification was complete, it fell to the new king to accompany the embalmed body to Thebes in early August for interment in the Valley of the Kings, in what is the longest and most spectacular tomb ever excavated in the royal necropolis.

The timing was fortunate, as it enabled Ramesses II to participate personally in the annual Festival of the Sanctuary. This was the occasion every year when the cult statue of Amun-Ra, Egypt's chief deity, was taken in procession from its usual resting place in the temple of Karnak to the god's "southern sanctuary" (the ancient Egyptian designation for Luxor Temple). While the god rested and recuperated from his pressing duties — ancient Egyptian deities, like their later Greek counterparts, were believed to have human needs and desires — the reigning monarch could take the opportunity to visit Amun-Ra in the private apartments at the back of the temple. There the divine essence (*ka*) of kingship was recharged by close communion with the god, allowing the king to emerge into the temple forecourt visibly rejuvenated as "foremost of all the living kas."[17] It was an elaborate piece of royal and religious theater, designed, like so much of ancient Egyptian ritual, to emphasize the divinity of kingship. The Festival of the Sanctuary had been invented at the beginning of the eighteenth dynasty, when the royal family felt the need to burnish its credentials after the humiliating experience of foreign invasion and civil war. For centuries afterward, the festival offered the perfect symbolic setting for the start of a reign, and it would not have escaped Ramesses' notice that Horemheb, the nineteenth dynasty's godfather, had used the self-same festival as the occasion for his coronation.

The ceremonies at Luxor duly accomplished, Ramesses left Thebes in mid-September ("Year 1, third month of the inundation season, day twenty-three" in the Egyptian calendar) and sailed downstream, bound for Avaris. With heavy symbolism, his first stop en route was Abydos. There he appointed a new high priest of Amun, Nebwenenef, presenting him with two gold signet rings and a staff of office before sending him south to take up his appointment at Karnak. But buildings, not people, seem to have been uppermost in Ramesses' mind. According to a later retrospective inscription, when he inspected his father's great dynastic temple, Ramesses found a troubling state of affairs: "Now the Mansion of Menmaatra, its front and back, were in the course of construction when he entered heaven. Its dedication had not been completed, the pillars had not been erected on its terrace, and its cult image [still] lay upon the ground, having not [yet] been fashioned in the proper manner of the goldsmiths' workshop. Its offerings had ceased, and the staff of the temple likewise."[18] While pharaohs in general, and Ramesses II in particular, were given to exaggeration and hyperbole in their inscriptions, in this case the account seems to be a true one. The rear part of Seti I's Abydos temple was indeed finished by Ramesses and his successors, and the pillars of the portico were entirely decorated by Ramesses, as were the two courts and the pylon in front of the hypostyle hall. Epigraphic evidence clearly dates these building phases to the early part of Ramesses II's sole reign, sometime after his second year on the throne.

Elsewhere at Abydos, the picture was equally bleak. Visiting the royal necropolis of Egypt's earliest rulers, Ramesses "found the memorial chapels of the kings of the past and their stelae which were in Abydos fallen into abandonment, half of them still in the process of [re]construction." Conscious of his recent accession, and of the corresponding need to show himself the true heir of Seti I (and the true inheritor of all his royal predecessors), Ramesses seized the opportunity to restore, complete, and beautify the monuments of earlier kings at Abydos. In his own words, "The Lord of the Two Lands arose as king to act as Champion of His Father during Year 1."[19]

While there are references to the dedication of statues of the late Seti I in Thebes and Memphis, it was at Abydos that Ramesses concentrated his early efforts. It is no coincidence that the most extensive surviving text from Ramesses II's long reign is his Great Dedicatory Inscription at Abydos. It may conflate more than one visit to the site, but it paints a vivid picture of a king intent on fulfilling his destiny. Though dated to Ramesses' early years on the throne, the inscription can be read as the credo for his entire reign.

At the heart of its message is the king's relationship with his late father, and his determination to prove himself a worthy heir. As Ramesses himself put it in the inscription, "I answer on behalf of my father, he being in the Netherworld."

After recounting his participation in the Festival of the Sanctuary and his journey from Thebes, Ramesses describes his reason for visiting Abydos ("In order to see his father"), his arrival at the site, and his discovery of the ruinous state of Seti I's temple. Intent upon restoring order and honoring his forebears, the king summons his officials, who deliver a lengthy eulogy to the new sovereign. Their words are formulaic, reflecting the grandiloquent language that attended an Egyptian pharaoh at every turn: "You are Ra. Your body is his body. There has never been a[nother] ruler like you, for you are unique, like the son of Osiris. You have performed the [very] model of his plans." Next, Ramesses announces his intention of completing his father's monument, so that "it will be said, forever and ever, 'It is his son who makes his name live.'" Then comes Ramesses' (embroidered) recollection of how he was elevated to the kingship while still a child and an enumeration of his works as co-regent. A second eulogy by the courtiers follows, after which the pharaoh summons craftsmen to start the restoration, alongside work on a suite of new buildings for Ramesses himself: "making monument upon monument, two benefactions at once, in my name and my father's name."

The closing sections of the inscription are the most personal, and perhaps allow a glimpse into Ramesses' own thoughts and motives at the start of his reign. First comes a heartfelt address by Ramesses to his late father:

> Behold, you have entered into heaven, you follow the sun, you have
> joined the stars and the moon. You are at peace in the underworld, like

its inhabitants, at the side of Wennefer [Osiris], lord of eternity. Your arms pull Atum in the sky and on earth, like the unwearying, imperishable stars, since you are in the prow of the bark of millions. When Ra rises in heaven, your eyes behold his beauty. When Atum enters the [under]world, you are among his followers. You have entered the hidden chamber in the presence of its master. You range widely inside the underworld. You fraternize with the gods of the necropolis.

Ramesses promises, as long as he remains king, to restore and maintain his father's monuments and offerings. Then follows Seti's response, "rejoicing for everything his son had done," and promising intercession with the gods on his son's behalf:

Happiness and rejoicing shall be in your every place, O king who protects Egypt, who binds the foreign lands. You will spend the eternity of your lifetime as divine king and ruler, while Atum flourishes at [his] rising and setting. Behold, I say to Ra with a loving heart, "Grant him an eternity upon earth like Khepri [the god of the rising sun]." I repeat to Osiris when I enter into his presence, "Double for him the lifetime of your son Horus." Behold, Ra says in the horizon of heaven, "Grant everlastingness, eternity, and millions of jubilees to the son of his body, the beloved Ramesses, beloved of Amun, given life, who performs benefactions."

Seti's closing remarks to his son were both a prayer and a prophecy: "The Southland and the Northland are beneath thy feet, beseeching millions of jubilees for Usermaatra, Ra's chosen one."

It was not only at Abydos that the young Ramesses II seemed determined to live up to his father's expectations and follow in his footsteps. Another visit in the first year of the new reign took the pharaoh to the sandstone quarries at Gebel el-Silsila to leave a commemorative inscription in the place where Seti I had carried out notable works. Not long afterward another of the late king's achievements, in the gold-mining district of the Eastern Desert, came to his son's mind: "One day it came to pass that His Majesty was sitting upon the Electrum Throne, crowned with the double-plumed diadem, thinking about the foreign lands from which gold is brought, and devising plans for digging wells along the routes without water, after hearing that there was abundant gold in the land of Akuyati but that its route was lacking in water. Hence no gold was brought from this country for lack of water." The viceroy of Kush—the king's personal representative in conquered Nubia and adjacent regions—was duly summoned and explained the situation: "Every king of the past desired to dig a well there, but to no avail. The late king Menmaatra did likewise, and in his time had a well dug 120 cubits in depth, but it lies abandoned along the road, for no water came from it." Far from being downhearted, if the inscription is to be believed, Ramesses decreed that a new well should be dug in a different location; and hey presto! "Water came forth from it at [a depth of just] 12 cubits." It was duly named "The Well, Ramesses II valiant in deeds." Whatever its historical veracity, in this text, dated to Ramesses' third year on the throne, we witness the new king's personal transformation: no longer content merely to match his father's accomplishments, he was now determined to exceed them.[20]

Two visible changes accompanied the king's coming of age. The first was a small but highly significant addition to his throne name. At the start of his reign, he had chosen the straightforward Usermaatra, occasionally embellished with an additional epithet such as "image of Ra" or "heir of Ra." But some time before the end of his second regnal year, he formally added the epithet "Ra's chosen one" (*setepenra*) to his throne name. Ramesses son of Seti thus became Ramesses elect of the creator god. For the rest of his long reign, monuments would celebrate Usermaatra-setepenra, harking back to the days of the pyramid builders, when kings had likewise claimed direct authority from the sun god.

The second change was in the style of carving on temple walls. Seti I's monuments had been characterized by the use of raised relief, whereby the entire background of a scene was cut away, leaving the figures and hieroglyphs standing clear of the surface. The results were visually stunning — Seti's work remains among the finest ever accomplished in ancient Egypt — but hugely labor-intensive and time-consuming. Ramesses, having watched both his grandfather and his father enjoy only comparatively short reigns, knew from personal experience that death could come at any moment. He was a king in a hurry and had ambitious plans for new construction projects the length and breadth of Egypt. He therefore needed a quicker alternative to raised relief for his planned decorative programs. His craftsmen switched, almost overnight, to the technique of sunk relief, whereby each figure or character was "sunk" into its own small area of the surface, leaving the rest of the background untouched. It speeded up the process of decoration enormously, even if the aesthetic result was less pleasing.

Thanks to these two innovations, the monuments from the early part of Ramesses' reign can be dated quite precisely. The first phase, employing raised relief and the early form of throne name, can be attributed to the co-regency of Ramesses and his father. The second phase, characterized by sunk relief but retaining the early form of the throne name, can be dated to Ramesses' first year or two of sole rule. And the third phase, which lasted for the rest of his reign, employed sunk relief and the later form of his throne name. Consequently, we know that the majority of the work to complete Seti I's temple at Abydos was carried out after Ramesses' second year, which suggests that he spent his first year or so focusing on his own monuments at the site. By contrast, completion of Seti I's memorial temple at western Thebes (present-day Qurna), including construction of the entrance portico, began as soon as Ramesses acceded to the throne.

So much for the completion of Seti's unfinished projects. A king's duty was not merely to be a good son and heir by championing his father's legacy: it was also to leave a legacy of his own. And so, on leaving Abydos in the first year of his reign, Ramesses headed north, to his family's hometown in the northeastern Delta, intent upon just such a project to propitiate the gods and proclaim his own power.

THE HOUSE OF RAMESSES

The town of Avaris, seat of the Ramesside dynasty, had something of a checkered history.[21] It had been founded in the late third millennium B.C. as a border post, its inhabitants helping to settle and secure a vulnerable yet strategically important part of Egypt's frontier with Palestine. In the twelfth dynasty, Avaris had formed part of the Walls of the Ruler, a series of defensive fortifications established along the eastern Delta margins to keep out marauding Bedouins and Asiatic immigrants. But these defenses had proved ill-equipped to deal with an unstoppable tide of economic migrants from the parched lands of the Near East; over the course of a few generations, in the late twelfth and thirteenth dynasties, these foreign peoples had infiltrated Egyptian territory, set up their own communities, and even appointed their own leaders — all under the noses of an increasingly strained and ineffective Egyptian administration. When central authority finally broke down under the weight of pressures from within and without, the leaders of Avaris had proclaimed themselves kings, adopted the trappings of pharaonic authority, and gone on to rule the entire Nile Delta (and much of the Nile Valley) for a period of a hundred years.

For much of the so-called Second Intermediate Period (c. 1630–1539 B.C.), these "rulers of foreign lands" (*hekau-khasut* in ancient Egyptian, *Hyksos* in the more familiar Greek form) dominated Egypt. Their rule saw aspects of Levantine culture—notably, gods such as Baal, and technology such as the horse and chariot—introduced into the Nile Valley. Eventually, the ancestors of the eighteenth dynasty, by adopting Asiatic weapons of war for themselves, were able to launch a campaign of liberation to drive the Hyksos out of Egypt. The establishment of an Egyptian empire in the Near East had been one consequence of this campaign, its primary purpose to act as buffer territory against any future invasion. As for Avaris, once the Hyksos had been driven out, their capital was rebuilt as a base for Egyptian troops, reverting to its original role as a border post.

Hence Ramesses II's forebears had grown up in a town with strong military connections and powerful associations, both positive and negative, with the neighboring lands of the Near East. At the heart of Avaris, the Hyksos temple to Baal had been "sanitized" and integrated into pharaonic religious practice by rededicating it to the Egyptian warrior god Seth. An intriguing monument that may in some way commemorate this event is the so-called Stela of 400 Years, found at Tanis but originally set up at Avaris during Ramesses II's reign.[22] It shows the god Seth being worshipped by Ramesses and another man named as "Seti, son of Paramessu and Tia." The latter, who wears the ceremonial bull's tail of kingship but no other royal regalia, would seem to indicate the future Seti I (named after the god Seth) while he was still a commoner in the reign of Horemheb. The stela may recall an event presided over by Seti to commemorate the establishment of the cult of Seth at Avaris, or the initial rise to local prominence of the Ramesside royal family itself.

It was in the same town that Seti, as king, had established his summer residence, and where his son Ramesses may have spent a significant portion of his childhood. From the beginning of Ramesses' own reign, plans were developed to expand Avaris into a glittering royal residence, a seat of power worthy of a new dynasty. In the process, the name Avaris, with all its complicated associations, would be consigned to history. In its place would emerge a city to be called Per-Ramesses-mery-Amun-aa-nakhtu, "the House of Ramesses-beloved-of-Amun, Great of Victories." As a contemporary scribe wrote:

> His Majesty has built himself a residence whose name is "Great of
>   Victories";
> It lies between Syria and Egypt, full of food and provisions;
> It follows the model of Upper-Egyptian Thebes, its lifespan like that
>   of Memphis.
> The sun rises on its horizon and sets within it.
> Everyone has left his own town to settle in its precincts.[23]

The rediscovery and excavation of Per-Ramesses (present-day Qantir) since 1980 ranks as one of the great achievements of Egyptian archaeology.[24] Complementing small-scale excavations, geophysical techniques have uncovered much of the city's original plan. Covering an area of some 250 acres, with abundant fertile land in the vicinity, Per-Ramesses was a city of vast living quarters, with streets of small houses and large villas with their own gardens and private wells. It was also a city of waterways, which brought fresh water as well as providing for transport, irrigation, and defense. To the west and north of the settlement flowed the ancient Pelusiac branch of the Nile, known to the Egyptians as "the waters of Ra," while to the south and east was an artificial canal, "the waters of Avaris," which in turn fed a lake called "the waters of the Residence." Farther south, a second lake permitted the development of an inland port with direct access to both the Nile and the Mediterranean Sea. Per-Ramesses was thus a veritable ancient Egyptian Venice. Modern remote sensing has detected these ancient watercourses, lakebeds, and harbor, confirming the account of an early visitor named Pabasa who described the city in glowing terms: "It is a very beautiful place that, although it resembles Thebes, has no equal. . . . Life in the Residence is pleasant; its fields abound with all sorts of good produce; each day it is well endowed with good food. Its canals are filled with fish, and its marshlands with birds. . . . Its granaries are filled with barley and wheat."[25]

Another firsthand account of Per-Ramesses, preserved on papyrus, describes the city as divided into four quarters, each named after its local temple. In the south, and coinciding with the old town of Avaris, was the quarter of Seth, its temple incorporating much earlier twelfth-dynasty buildings. In the north, named after a temple to the tutelary goddess of Lower Egypt, was the quarter of Wadjet. The western quarter was dedicated to Amun (whose temple was the largest in the city, as befitted the state god), and the eastern quarter to the Asiatic deity Astarte. There were also temples to the god of Memphis, Ptah (in the northern quarter), and the god of Heliopolis, Ra-Horakhty (in the east).[26] Per-Ramesses was thus home to a diverse, multifaith community, characteristic of imperial Egypt in the nineteenth dynasty. Its numerous places of worship constituted perhaps the greatest collection of religious foundations ever built by a single ruler.

Between the temples of Amun and Ptah, next to the Waters of
Ra, stood a magnificent complex of buildings used for royal ceremonial. Called the Halls of Jubilee, in their final form they comprised two vast columned courtyards and associated chambers,
fronted by a granite gateway and at least three pairs of obelisks.
The hypostyle halls closely resemble the so-called Coronation
Hall at Akhenaten's capital city of Amarna and seem to reflect a
standard pattern for such buildings. What is distinctive about the
Halls of Jubilee at Per-Ramesses is their decoration: the palace
was adorned throughout with colored glass tiles, forming intricate
scenes on walls and columns. A chamber plausibly identified as
the throne room was decorated with tiled panels showing bound
captives, vassals paying tribute to the pharaoh, and lions eating
prisoners of war: all suitable subjects for creating an atmosphere
of absolute monarchical power. By contrast, the quarters allocated
to the royal women bore more subdued decoration: floral motifs
and aquatic scenes of fish and fowl. Another room in the palace
complex had a polychrome stucco floor with gold-plated elements.
Something of the exuberance of Akhenaten's art remained in the
widespread use of colored glass inlays, figurative tiles, and lush
composite columns. The overall impression must have been one
of unbounded wealth and luxury, as underscored in a contemporary description of a festival day: "The young people of 'Great of
Victories' are in festival-dress daily, with oil on their heads, hair
freshly set. They stand in their doorways, hands weighed down
with foliage and greenery . . . on the day of the ceremonial entry of
Ramesses."[27] The opulence of the royal palace continued beyond
its interior and into the grounds, which included ornamental plea-
sure gardens with a lake and a zoo. Bones found in the vicinity
suggest that the animals kept in captivity for the king's entertain-
ment included lions, elephants, and giraffes.

While the north of Per-Ramesses seems to have been the setting for major royal ceremonies, the entire city bore the unmistakable imprint of its pharaonic foundation. Every temple gateway and forecourt was filled with colossal statues of the king—at least fifty in total. Their purpose was to act as intermediaries between the people and the gods, as well as to provide a focus for popular worship in their own right.[28] Some of the statues had their own hereditary priesthoods and cult officials. Local inhabitants dedicated votive offerings to the statues, each of which bore a name: some of the monikers were complex theological formulations, such as "Usermaatra-setepenra who is effective for Seth" or "Montu of the Two Lands" (the latter seems to have been the most popular of all Ramesses' statue cults, attracting the attention of people of all social backgrounds, from untitled men and women to the high priest of Ra); some were more concise, such as "Appearing among the gods" or "Beloved of Atum"; others were short and to the point, such as "Son of rulers" or "Ruler of rulers." One of the colossal statues of Ramesses II was named, simply, "The God." In the House of Ramesses, religious sentiment and loyalty to the crown were indivisible.

But Per-Ramesses was not just, or even principally, a residence city. It was, in origin and by design, a military base. This aspect of its character is best attested in the east of the city, close to the Temple of Astarte. The goddess, also known as Ishtar, was the chief female deity of the Levantine peoples (Canaanites and Phoenicians) and was associated with fertility, sexuality, and war. When her cult had been brought to Egypt during the imperial adventures of the eighteenth dynasty, she had been recast as patron deity of the chariotry and the royal horse team. It is fitting, therefore, that at Per-Ramesses, in the shadow of Astarte's temple, there was a royal stud with stabling for at least 460 horses. The portico had an inscription dedicating it to the goddess, while an accompanying relief showed the king standing before a statue of Astarte (depicted as a woman on horseback).

Alongside the stables were other buildings making up a huge chariotry garrison. There was a wide, pillared court for exercising the horses: the archaeological layers excavated here have even yielded hoofprints, preserved in the compacted soil for over three thousand years. Other finds include chariot finials, a pair of bridle bits, and yoke knobs. As well as housing the standard battle chariots, the complex also seems to have contained a workshop for the manufacture and repair of the lavish parade chariots used in royal spectacles (the ancient Egyptian equivalent of the state coaches and landaus used by some royal families today). Artifacts recovered through archaeology include nail heads covered with gold leaf, bands of gold with embossed decoration, gold-plated bronze buttons, and a once gilded linchpin. The more practical purpose of chariotry—as an instrument of war—is attested by discoveries of metal scales from body armor and examples of the weapons routinely deployed by Egyptian chariot officers: arrowheads, daggers, and lances.

The scale of Ramesses II's ambition at Per-Ramesses, and the wider military character of the city, is most spectacularly attested by the excavation of a huge bronze foundry, covering an area of more than seven acres. It is the largest known from the ancient world, and the only one to have deployed specialized, high-temperature furnaces for heating large-scale casting molds. Other finds from the site include all the paraphernalia of metalworking—crucibles, tuyeres, molds, scrap metal, recycled bronze objects, and pieces of slag—together with evidence for other industries: glassmaking and the production of inlays, stone vessel manufacture, and leatherworking. One area even specialized in the production of exotic bone objects, using material brought from the nearby royal zoo.

Ramesses' intention seems to have been to create a vast military-industrial complex, with all of the facilities required to equip and service an army. Within a few years of the beginning of his reign, his new city had become the most important military base in the country, as well as a ceremonial capital, royal residence, and flourishing entrepôt. Per-Ramesses was notably cosmopolitan, home to many different peoples from across the empire. Alongside the Egyptian state gods, the royal statue cults, and the officially sanctioned Levantine cult of Astarte, other Asiatic deities were worshipped: the Canaanite storm and fertility god Baal; his consort, the battle goddess Anat; the god of lightning and plague, Reshep; and Hauron, a protector deity against enemies both in this world and the next. The nature of all these cults reinforces the multicultural as well as the military character of Per-Ramesses. Moreover, the chariotry complex has yielded objects of foreign origin — pottery from the Aegean, Cyprus, the Levant, and Anatolia, and a scale from a boar's-tusk helmet of the type known to have been worn exclusively by high-ranking Mycenaean officials — indicating that foreign ambassadors stayed at Per-Ramesses, perhaps representatives of allied powers in Egypt's foreign campaigns. Foreigners are known to have served at the pharaoh's court as diplomatic envoys. The Egyptian army, too, had a number of foreign detachments, made up of mercenaries and former prisoners of war and their descendants, such as the Sherden pirates captured by Ramesses during his royal apprenticeship.

Hence, within a few years of ascending the throne, Ramesses II had built himself a dazzling military base-cum-imperial residence. Equipped with garrisons and chariotry stables, armaments factories and workshops, and host to representatives from foreign allies across the eastern Mediterranean, everything was set for the large-scale projection of Egyptian imperial power into the neighboring lands of the Levant. Where Seti I had led, his son was determined to follow. He would not have to wait long for the chance to prove himself.

CHAPTER TWO

War and Peace

The Kingdom of the Hittites had first come to Egypt's attention in the reign of Thutmose III, in the mid-eighteenth
dynasty, in the course of numerous campaigns in the Near East.[1]
At that point, Hatti (as the kingdom was known in Akkadian, the
diplomatic lingua franca of the age) was a relatively minor re-
gional power, largely confined to its heartland in central Anatolia.
But within a few generations, Hatti had extended its sphere of
influence down through Syria, challenging the Kingdom of Mittani for hegemony over the northern Levant. Amenhotep III, recognizing the advent of a new power and keen to defend Egypt's
interests in the region, had entered into diplomatic correspondence
with the ambitious king of the Hittites, Suppiluliuma, and may
even have signed a peace treaty to guarantee cordial relations. A
treaty was certainly signed between the two sides in the reign of
Akhenaten. That in turn led Egypt to withdraw its support from
Mittani, a long-standing ally of Egypt but a rival of Hatti. The
Hittites took full advantage of this opportunity: by the reign of
Tutankhamun, it was Hatti, not Mittani, that dominated much of

Syria. By playing power politics, Egypt had unwittingly created a strong rival and potential adversary in its own backyard.

Egyptian-Hittite relations then took a bizarre turn. Surviving texts from the Hittite royal annals record that when Tutankhamun died unexpectedly, his young widow, Ankhesenamun, being childless and vulnerable as the last surviving member of the eighteenth-dynasty royal family, wrote in desperation to Suppiluliuma, asking him to send one of his sons to Egypt to marry her and rule beside her. For, as she explained, "Never shall I take a servant of mine and make him my husband!"[2] After sending emissaries to Egypt to investigate this extraordinary request, the Hittite king apparently agreed, and promptly dispatched one of his sons to the Nile Valley—but the prince died en route, probably at the hands of an Egyptian assassin. War between the two powers nearly ensued, and Ankhesenamun disappeared from history, her fate unknown. The ultimate beneficiary of this whole episode was Tutankhamun's general and deputy (and no friend of the Hittites), Horemheb: in the absence of a natural-born heir, it was he who succeeded to the throne. There followed decades of strained relations between Egypt and Hatti, punctuated by periodic campaigns when one or the other power targeted its enemy's proxies, the vassal states of central and northern Syria. These states, for their part, played off the rival powers against each other, switching allegiance with dizzying rapidity to gain temporary advantage.

So the situation stood throughout most of Seti I's reign. A successful campaign to secure the loyalty of the southern Syrian province of Upe (the oasis of Damascus and the central Beqaa Valley) had shored up Egyptian influence in the region, but the key province of Amurru (coastal Lebanon and Syria north of Byblos, and the areas inland, straddling the Lebanon Range), which had formerly been loyal to Egypt, remained under Hittite control, threatening Egyptian access to Syria's Mediterranean ports. Also in Hittite hands was the strategic fortress of Kadesh, long a thorn in Egypt's side. Egypt and Hatti now squared up against each other, each determined to assert its hegemony.

A fragmentary inscription dating to Ramesses II's first few years as king indicates that the Moabites (who lived in the highlands east of the Dead Sea) had incurred the pharaoh's wrath because they had allied themselves with the Hittites; this suggests mounting Egyptian concern over Hittite domination of trade routes leading south via Kadesh.[3] Spurred on by such developments, Ramesses II was intent, from the beginning of his reign, upon completing Seti I's work and bringing Amurru back into the Egyptian fold. In his fourth year on the throne, 1275 B.C., Ramesses set out for Syria with a large army, equipped and prepared in the garrison at Per-Ramesses.[4] His force swept north, through the loyal Egyptian province of Canaan and up the coast, via the ports of Tyre and Byblos, as far as Simyra, to reaffirm Egyptian control of the eastern Mediterranean littoral. From Simyra, he struck inland via the Eleutheros (Nahr el-Kebir) Valley to attack Amurru, surprising its vassal ruler, Benteshina, and securing the province's pledge of loyalty. A humbled Benteshina wrote to his former overlord, King Muwatalli II of Hatti (grandson of Suppiluliuma), to relay the embarrassing news. The Hittites had no intention of accepting this loss of both face and territory. Over the succeeding months, Muwatalli prepared a large army of his own, bolstered by troops from allies and vassals, perhaps sixteen different contingents alongside the Hittite soldiers themselves:

> Now the vile enemy of Hatti had come and gathered to himself all the foreign lands as far as the farthest extent of the sea. The entire land of Hatti had come, Naharin likewise, Arzawa, Dardany, and Keshkesh,

those of Masa, Pidasa, Irun, Karkisha, Lukka, Kizzuwadna, Carchemish, Ugarit, and Kedy, the entire land of Nuges, Mushanet, and Kadesh. He had not spared a country from being brought, from all those distant lands; and their chiefs were with him, each with his infantry and chariotry, a vast multitude without equal. They covered the mountains and valleys like a multitude of locusts. He had left no silver in his land but had stripped it of all its wealth, giving it to all the foreign lands to bring them along with him to fight.[5]

Later accounts put the size of the Hittite force at thirty-seven thousand men and twenty-five hundred chariots. If this figure is even moderately accurate, it points to one of the biggest standing armies ever levied in the Bronze Age world.

The Egyptians were not unaware of the forces being massed against them. In the spring months of Ramesses II's fifth regnal year, 1274, the preparations at Per-Ramesses must have been frenzied, as the pharaoh amassed his own forces, intent upon defending his recent conquest of Amurru and seeing off the Hittite threat. The army at his disposal was some twenty thousand strong, comprising four divisions, each a mix of infantry and chariotry, drawn from the different parts of Egypt and bolstered, if not dominated, by foreign mercenaries. Each division was named after a patron deity. The lead division, that of Amun, may have been recruited largely from Thebes; next came the division of Ra, levied from the area around Heliopolis, but including an auxiliary unit of Palestinian vassals; then the division of Ptah, from the Memphite region; and in the rearguard, the division of Seth, recruited from the immediate vicinity of Per-Ramesses.

At the beginning of April 1274, when the last of the winter snows had begun to melt in Anatolia and the highlands of Syria, everything was prepared for battle: "Now His Majesty had prepared his infantry and his chariotry, and the Sherden in His Majesty's captivity whom he had brought back through the victories of his sword arm. Supplied with all their arms, battle orders had been given to them. His Majesty journeyed north, his infantry and chariotry with him, having made a good start with the march, in year 5, second month of the summer season, day 9."[6] The army soon passed the Egyptian border fortress of Tjaru (Tell Hebua), after which it entered potentially hostile territory.

The elaborate preparations taken for its safe passage are illustrated at the recently excavated site of Tell Abyad, on the western edge of the Sinai peninsula, not far from ancient Egypt's northeastern border.[7] There a large mudbrick building has been discovered, covering an area of some twenty-seven thousand square feet, set within an enclosure wall six feet thick. Around the perimeter of the complex are traces of a fortified entrance gateway, perhaps surrounded by a moat or second enclosure wall. Fragments of painted plaster show that some of the rooms were originally brightly colored, with a decorative scheme including garlands of flowers and a red, white, and blue cornice. Such features tend to indicate a royal residence, while the architecture of the building as a whole suggests a fortification, constructed rapidly (the foundations are shallow, despite the building's size) and used for a comparatively short period of time. Tell Abyad may have served as a campaign headquarters, perhaps a staging post for one of Ramesses II's military offensives in the Near East. The pottery found at the site confirms a date early in the king's reign.

Besides the soldiers themselves, the Egyptian expeditionary force would have consisted of horses and chariots, pack animals and carts laden with materiel and provisions, logistics and support personnel, the king's chief advisers, and even members of the royal family. (Princes, on reaching the age of puberty, were expected, as

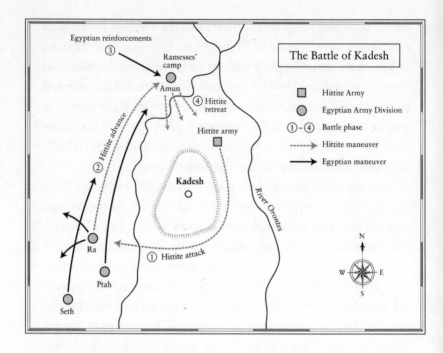

The Battle of Kadesh

Hittite Army
Egyptian Army Division
①–④ Battle phase
Hittite maneuver
Egyptian maneuver

Egyptian reinforcements
③ Ramesses' camp
Amun
④ Hittite retreat
Hittite army
Kadesh
Hittite advance
②
River Orontes
Ra
① Hittite attack
Ptah
Seth
N W E S

Ramesses had, to participate in military campaigns, albeit at a safe distance from the front line.) Such a large army moved relatively slowly, covering 13 to 15 miles per day. From the northern Sinai, the Egyptian force marched north through the province of Canaan with its administrative capital of Gaza, to the west of the Sea of Galilee, through the hill country of Lebanon and the Beqaa Valley (known to the Egyptians as "the valley of cedar"), via the Upe provincial capital of Kumidi (Kamid el-Loz), and on toward its final destination, the contested city of Kadesh. The whole journey, a distance of some 420 miles, took exactly a month.

On May 1, 1274, the vanguard of the Egyptian army cleared the "wood of Labwi" (el-Labwe), about 10 miles south of Kadesh, and proceeded to ford the Orontes. Shortly after the division of Amun had crossed over to the west bank of the river, the king's guard announced a stroke of luck: they had intercepted two Bedouins hiding in the trees. On interrogation, the men claimed to be deserters from the Hittite army and swore allegiance to the pharaoh. Moreover, they reported that the main Hittite force was still 120 miles away to the north, in the area of Aleppo, and reluctant to engage in a full-scale pitched battle with the Egyptians. Ramesses' army could not believe its luck. The king, riding at the head of the division of Amun, pressed on across the plain and set up camp on high ground to the northwest of Kadesh. The divisions of Ra, Ptah, and Seth were following behind, each strung out over a distance of three-quarters of a mile.

As the king and his advance guard rested in their camp, two more Hittite spies were captured and tortured for information. Their story was very different, and alarming: "His Majesty said to them, 'Where is he, that enemy from Hatti? I had heard that he was in the land of Aleppo, to the north of Tunip.' They said to His Majesty, 'Look, the vile chief of Hatti has already come, together with the many countries that are supporting him, whom he has brought as allies. . . . They are equipped with their infantry and their chariotry, with their weapons of war. They are more numerous than the sand on the shore. Look, they stand ready to fight, behind Old Kadesh.'"[8] The two Bedouins captured earlier in the day had been Hittite spies, deliberately sent to spread misinformation. The Hittite force was not 120 miles away; it was encamped just behind Kadesh in the ruins of the old city, out of sight. Ramesses' army had marched into a trap.

According to the official account, the king's immediate reaction was to summon his officers for an emergency council of war. In what seems a highly likely description of events, Ramesses blamed his subordinates for the blunder, while they blamed faulty intelligence. Wherever the responsibility lay, the vulnerability of the Egyptian army was clear for all to see. Quick action was needed if the Egyptian force were not to be annihilated before the battle had even begun. As soon as it became clear that an advance squadron of Hittite chariots was already bearing down on the royal camp, the first response was to send the accompanying members of the royal family to a safe place. At the same time, the vizier and military messengers were dispatched to warn and summon the three remaining army divisions, which were still approaching from the south. However, while the division of Ra was crossing the plain in full sight, it was attacked from the east by a force of Hittite chariotry which had swept down and around Kadesh, unseen by the Egyptians until it was too late. The pharaoh's terrified soldiers scattered, some of the chariots fleeing north toward the royal camp — inadvertently leading the enemy directly to the king's location.

As Hittite shock troops — "three men to a chariot and equipped with all the weapons of war" — stormed into the Egyptian battle headquarters along its western side, members of the division of Amun fled in all directions, leaving their commander-in-chief dangerously isolated. But Ramesses, who must have felt that Kadesh was his rendezvous with destiny, claims to have been inspired by the god Amun to stand his ground and fight:

> There was no officer with me, no charioteer,
> No solider of the army, no shield bearer.
> My infantry and my chariotry ran away before them [the enemy];
> Not one of them stood firm to fight with them. . . .
>
> I call to you, my father Amun,
> For I am in the midst of a multitude of strangers;
> All foreign lands are united against me;

I am all alone and there is nobody with me!

My great army has deserted me;

Not one of my chariotry looks out for me.

I keep shouting for them,

But none of them heeds my call.

I believe that Amun helps me, more than a million troops,

More than hundreds of thousands of charioteers,

More than ten thousand brothers and sons,

United as one heart. . . .

Although I prayed in a distant land,

My prayer resounded in Thebes.

I found that Amun came when I called to him;

He gave me his hand and I rejoiced.

He called from behind as if face to face. . . .

I shot on my right, grasped [the bowstring] with my left,

I was before them [the enemy] like Seth in his moment.

I found the twenty-five hundred chariots surrounding me,

Scattering before my horses.

Not one of them found his hand to fight.

Their hearts failed within them through fear of me.[9]

There is, of course, a strong element of hyperbole in the official account. In fact, what saved the Egyptians from a crushing defeat was a combination of good luck and good planning—a quick-witted, tactical response to an initial tactical blunder. Their lucky break came when the Hittite forces abandoned all discipline and began looting the equipment of the scattered division of Ra, in premature anticipation of complete victory. At the same time, an elite Egyptian division, drawn "from all the leaders of his army," that had been detached from the main army with instructions to approach Kadesh from the west, arrived on the scene in the nick of time to attack the Hittite troops in the rear. The sudden appearance of fresh, well-trained troops caught the Hittites by surprise, and the Egyptians were able to push their foe back across the Orontes, where they collided head-on with Hittite reinforcements marching into battle. The result was utter confusion and panic among Egypt's enemies. In Ramesses' description of events, "I made them plunge into the water like crocodiles."[10]

Toward sunset, the Egyptian division of Ptah finally arrived (the division of Seth would not reach camp until the following day), allowing three-quarters of the pharaoh's army to regroup, take stock, and prepare for the morrow. Egyptian scribes tallied up the enemy dead by counting their severed left hands, while Ramesses harangued the troops who had deserted him, accusing them of weakness, cowardice, and disloyalty. At dawn the next day, in a brutal display of ruthless military discipline (and the earliest attested example of the practice known to the Romans as *decimatio*), Ramesses made an example of the worst offenders, the cowardly troops of the Amun division. Branding them "rebels,"

> My Majesty overpowered them;
> I slew them without sparing them;
> They sprawled before my horses
> And lay slain in bloodied heaps,

all in full view of the horror-struck Hittite army. A subsequent attack by Egyptian chariotry on the main Hittite camp inflicted some casualties but failed to deal a decisive blow. What became clear as the second day of hostilities wore on was that neither side wanted a full-scale pitched battle. Both sides had suffered losses, and neither could be sure of winning. The Battle of Kadesh ended in stalemate.[11] A cessation of hostilities was agreed upon, and both armies departed, each claiming victory. In fact, it was a strategic defeat for the Egyptians. Ramesses II never achieved his objective of securing the permanent allegiance of Amurru, less still of regaining Kadesh.

MYTHMAKING

The reason why it is possible to describe the Battle of Kadesh in such detail is because on returning home to Egypt, Ramesses II set about presenting the encounter as a famous victory. In a propaganda campaign of unprecedented scale and scope, a veil was drawn over the political failure – the loss to the Hittites not just of Amurru (Benteshina had been deposed and marched off to Hatti to explain his treachery) but also of Upe (where Muwatalli installed his brother Hattusili as governor). Instead, in word and image, the king's heroism in saving the day for the Egyptians, despite the failings and outright cowardice of his army, was trumpeted as the crowning event of the reign. The highly sanitized account of the Battle of Kadesh became, in effect, a new official creed. Within three or four years of the events themselves, the approved version began to circulate, written on papyrus and carved on temple walls. At Karnak a great tableau with extended captions depicting the battle took pride of place on the south exterior wall of the hypostyle hall, adding to – or even overshadowing – the accounts of Seti I's military exploits. At Luxor, the Battle of Kadesh was depicted no fewer than three times, including on the exterior wall of the entrance pylon, where it could be seen and admired by the general population. Versions were also included in the decorative scheme of Ramesses' memorial temple in western Thebes, at temples in distant Nubia, and at Abydos, the holiest and most significant of nineteenth-dynasty constructions.

In a demonstration of the ancient Egyptian genius for propaganda, the mythologized events of Kadesh were transformed into not one but two different compositions. The first was a pictorial record with extended captions. Large-scale battle scenes were a nineteenth-dynasty innovation, pioneered by Seti I for the decoration of Karnak and adopted with enthusiasm by his son. The reliefs illustrating the Battle of Kadesh are at first sight rather conventional, but they include elements which demonstrate a capacity for innovation found even among Egyptian artists steeped in centuries of tradition.

The tableaux focus on two localities. The first depicts the Egyptian camp, scene of Ramesses' heroic stand. On the left, chariots are prepared and horses groomed, ready for the battle. The king, enthroned and accompanied by his fan bearers, gestures toward his officials, who bring him the unwelcome news of the Hittite army's unexpected proximity. In the lowest register of the composition, members of the king's elite Sherden bodyguard, with their round shields and distinctive horned helmets, form a protective wall around the sovereign. A tiny vignette shows the two Hittite spies having confessions beaten out of them by stick-wielding Egyptians. The middle of the tableau depicts the elements of the camp itself: tents at the center within an enclosure, horses and materiel carefully arranged, boys and pack animals bringing supplies – even the king's pet lion, tethered at a safe distance from the tents – with the whole compound encircled by a wall of shields. But this composition of structure and order is invaded and disturbed by an unruly mass of Hittite chariots. Depicted at the center of the entire composition, this striking visual contrast serves as a shorthand for the whole incident and gives it a cosmic significance: the forces of order (the Egyptians) are threatened by the forces of chaos (the Hittites). At the right side of the tableau, the Egyptian relief force arrives to save the day. The serried ranks of the pharaoh's chariotry and infantry stand in marked and deliberate contrast to the pell-mell of Hittite troops.

The second tableau focuses on the field of battle. It is dominated on the left by a representation of Kadesh encircled by a loop of the River Orontes. A detachment of Hittite infantry marches out of the town, weapons brandished and standards flying, while other soldiers remain behind, stationed on the battlements. At the bottom of the scene more Hittite troops are marshaled, ready for battle, while all around the town the Hittite chariotry, three men to a chariot, drives out to engage the Egyptians. On the right of the scene, the central figure is that of Ramesses II in his royal chariot, drawing his bowstring to fire at the oncoming melee. (He seems to have had a penchant for this particular imagery: on a stela erected at Giza in the first year of his reign, he is described as pursuing his enemies "swifter than an arrow from the bow.")[12] While the Hittite chariots at top and bottom are shown in orderly squadrons, around the king they are scattered in disordered heaps, the bodies of men and horses alike sprawled, twisted, and prostrate beneath the king's steeds. At the center of the composition, a tiny detail adds local color and situates the tableau in time and space: a soldier of the Hittite army being pulled out of the river by his comrades standing on the opposite bank.

The pictorial representations of the battle thus serve multiple purposes: to contrast the discipline of the Egyptians with the unruliness of their enemies; to reference the king's cosmic role in defending created order; and, of course, to highlight the poise and bravery of Ramesses himself. Prominently displayed in so many

The Battle of Kadesh: A confused mass of Hittite troops falls prostrate before the rearing forelegs of Ramesses' chariot horses in the Ramesseum (author photo).

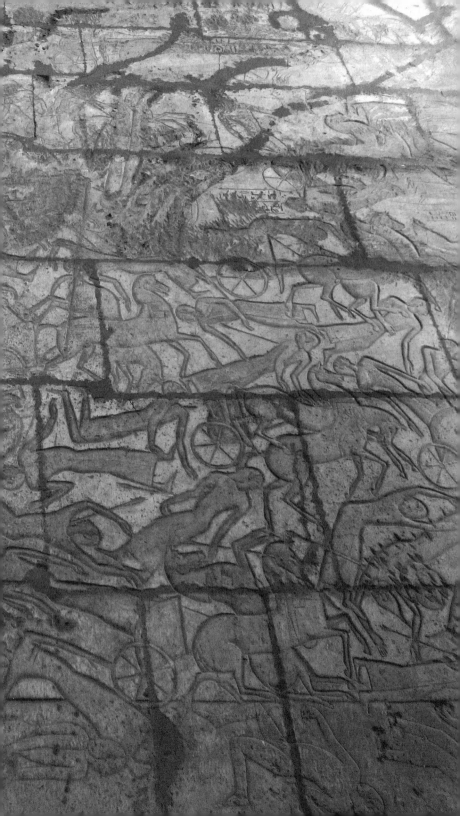

prime locations throughout the Nile Valley, the Kadesh battle reliefs would have made a powerful and lasting impression. The compositions are bold and distinctive, and their exotic details — the Orontes with its great bend, the walled town of Kadesh with its crenellations, the Hittite forces with their figure-of-eight shields — must have piqued the curiosity of all who saw them.

Accompanying the two tableaux is a set of extended captions dubbed by modern scholars "The Bulletin." It provides a good deal of detail on the events leading up to the battle; but in its description of the actual military encounter it presents a highly biased account, focusing on the king's professed heroism. The Bulletin begins with the capture of the two Bedouin agents and their misinformation about the Hittite army's whereabouts. What is striking is the length of description — some thirty lines — devoted to the deception. Indeed, the Bulletin rather belabors the point: "Now the two Bedouins who said these words were lying to His Majesty, for it was the Hittite enemy who had sent them to spy on where His Majesty was. . . . For the enemy of Hatti had come with his infantry and chariotry — and with the chiefs of every land that was in Hittite territory, and *their* infantry and chariotry, whom he had brought with him as allies to fight against His Majesty's army — and stood equipped and ready behind Old Kadesh; and His Majesty did not know that they were there." The effect is to build up the suspense and uncertainty about how the Egyptians will fare, in order to provide a foil for Ramesses' own bravery to come. Indeed, the Bulletin does not shy away from harsh criticism of the most senior Egyptian officials: "It is a great crime that the overseers of foreign lands and officials of Pharaoh have committed in failing to discover the enemy of Hatti wherever he was and reporting it to Pharaoh daily."[13] The trope of the wise king triumphing despite inept advisers (known by the German term *Königsnovelle*) was an old one in Egyptian literature. But the Bulletin took it to a new level, castigating the pharaoh's closest advisers in terms that would have been unthinkable to previous generations. The Bulletin may thus provide an insight into Ramesses II's character, or at least into the techniques of his spin doctors.

The last part of the Bulletin focuses on the pharaoh's legendary resistance to the surrounding foe. It is full of the sort of metaphor and hyperbole that had been used to describe the actions of Egyptian kings since time immemorial: "All his ground was ablaze with fire; he burned every country with his flame. His eyes were savage as he beheld them; his might burned with fire against them. . . . His Majesty was like Seth, great of strength, like Sekhmet in the moment of her rage." The final lines, however, return to the new Ramesside myth of the king *contra mundum:* "I attacked all the foreign lands, I alone. For my infantry and chariotry had deserted me; not one of them looked back." And to emphasize the veracity of the myth, the Bulletin ends with the king's sworn oath: "As I live, as Ra loves me, and as my father Atum praises me, everything My Majesty has said, I did it, in truth." Perhaps Ramesses truly believed his own story. In any case, nobody would have dared contradict such a royal assertion.

To accompany the Bulletin, the scribes of the Egyptian royal court composed a much longer account, combining prose narrative with lengthy interludes of metrical poetry. Egyptologists have dubbed it "The Poem," and it is indeed the earliest known occurrence in ancient Egyptian literature of an extended epic poem. Once again the central theme of the work is the king's heroism; in the Poem, its description extends to some 220 lines. The poetry takes the form of short lines of symmetrically structured speech with grammatical devices used to give the verse its meter, tempo, and coherence. A short prose introduction provides the "factual" background to the Battle of Kadesh, followed by an extended paean of praise to the pharaoh's many qualities. This is of traditional form, relying on a multiplicity of similes comparing Ramesses to the gods, wild beasts, and natural phenomena:

> His Majesty was a youthful master,
> Vigorous and without equal;
> His arms strong, his heart stout,
> His strength like Montu in his moment.
> Perfect of form like Atum,
> Hailed when his perfection is seen;
> Great of victories over all lands,
> Who does not hesitate to fight.
> Strong wall around his army,
> Their shield on the day of battle;
> Archer without equal,
> Who prevails over hundreds of thousands. . . .
> Steadfast in counsel, good in planning.
> Whose first response finds the spot,
> Who saves his army on the day of battle,
> And brings great aid to his charioteers;
> Brings home his followers, rescues his troops.
> Whose heart is like a copper mountain.[14]

Another prose section follows which relates the main events of the battle, up to the entry of the Hittite chariots into the Egyptian royal camp. This provides the background for the heart of the work, the epic poem celebrating the king's legendary achievements: the desertion of his troops, his appeal to Amun, the god's reply, the king's divinely inspired strength and resolution, the rout of the Hittite forces, Ramesses' lengthy tirade against his officers and soldiers, and his final victory against enemies and rebels alike. To the modern reader, the Poem comes across as repetitious ad nauseam, especially in the section (extending to one hundred lines of verse) in which Ramesses contrasts his bravery with his men's cowardice. But like most ancient Egyptian texts, it was composed to be recited aloud, and its heaping on of metaphor after metaphor must have had a powerful impact on an audience:

> How weak are your hearts, my charioteers;
> None among you is trustworthy! . . .
> But look, you have all been cowards;
> Not one person among you stood fast
> To give me a hand while I fought! . . .
> For not one among you has come
> That he might speak of his commission in the land of Egypt!
> What a good deed to him who raised monuments
> In Thebes, city of Amun,
> Is this crime committed by my infantry and chariotry
> That is too great to tell!

Again, what is interesting is the choice of emphasis. The Poem could have focused on the king's strategic genius: his decision while en route to Kadesh to detach an elite force, its orders to follow a different route north and rendezvous with the main Egyptian army ahead of the set-piece battle. Instead, the Poem extols the king's character — his quick thinking and bravery under fire — in contrast to the cravenness of his advisers and troops. This emphasis must have been deliberate, to elevate the pharaoh by belittling his own people and highlight his bond of trust with the gods (Amun in particular) in contrast to the disloyalty of his own troops. As a propaganda tactic it would not have been deployed, or at least not to such a degree, by earlier generations of Egyptian rulers. As a reflection of Ramesses' self-image, the Poem may be the closest we have to autobiographical evidence.

At the end of the composition, in what must be a brazen distortion of the facts, the Hittite ruler sends Ramesses a letter, suing for peace: "Be not hard in your dealings, victorious king! Peace is more effective than war. Let us breathe!" The king, magnanimous in victory, consults with his army, who are too afraid to gainsay him: "Then they said with one voice, 'Peace is indeed excellent, O sovereign our lord! There is no shame in peace when *you* make it; for who could resist you on the day of your wrath?'" Ramesses duly returns to Egypt, "the gods of this land embracing him and saying, 'Welcome, our beloved son.'" To set the seal on his famous victory, the gods of Egypt "granted him millions of jubilees forever upon the throne of Ra, all lands and all countries lying prostrate under his sandals forever and ever."

In sum, the official account of the Battle of Kadesh is a highly sophisticated example of mythmaking. Through word and image, a military encounter with no clear winner — and, moreover, a strategic defeat for the Egyptians — was recast as a heroic encounter, a personal victory for Ramesses, and the defining moment of his kingship. It was a myth to which he would return and upon which he would build for the rest of his reign.

FAR FRONTIERS

The Hittites and their allies on the northeastern fringes of the Egyptian empire were not the only threat with which Ramesses had to contend in order to ensure the peace and prosperity of his realm. Throughout Egyptian history, the fertile Nile Valley, with its abundant fresh water and productive fields, had attracted the covetous attention of peoples from the less prosperous lands to the south and west, too. Nubia—the stretch of valley south of the First Nile Cataract, where an impossibly narrow strip of irrigated land made subsistence particularly challenging—had been a thorn in Egypt's side since prehistoric times. Subsequent generations of Egyptian rulers, starting before the first dynasty and continuing to the eighteenth, had been compelled to launch periodic campaigns to subjugate and pacify the peoples of Nubia. Under Thutmose III, all of Nubia as far south as the Fourth Nile Cataract had been brought under Egyptian control, and the territory had remained largely peaceful to Ramesses II's time. Nubia was vital to Egypt as its main source of gold, and maintaining regular supplies of ore from the mines of the Nubian desert was a chief preoccupation of the Egyptian government. The pharaoh's representative in Nubia, the viceroy of Kush, was in charge of the entire administration of Egypt's southern province, but his primary concern was gold. It was to defend Egypt's economic interests in Nubia that Seti I had launched a campaign against Kush in his eighth regnal year, and the same motive no doubt lay behind the suppression of a minor revolt by Ramesses when he was crown prince. A further show of force seems to have been necessary sometime in Ramesses' second decade on the throne. Once again, this was left to the royal princes to oversee, giving them their first taste of battle; once again, Egyptian victory was never in doubt, and Nubia remained quiescent for decades to come. With Egyptian garrisons stationed throughout subject territory and easy riverine communication along the Nile, maintaining pharaonic domination of the southern lands posed little strategic challenge. The Bedouin nomads and restive city-states of Syria-Palestine on Egypt's northeastern border were altogether more troublesome and unpredictable, and this (along with dynastic ties) explains why Ramesses built his new residence and military-industrial complex at Per-Ramesses.

That left Egypt's long western frontier as the country's area of greatest vulnerability. Despite the bleak terrain and apparently inhospitable conditions of the Libyan Desert, the region had since prehistoric times supported a transhumant population of pastoralists. Given various names in the Egyptian sources — Tjehenu and Tjemeh were the most common — these tribespeople followed their herds from oasis to oasis according to the seasons, occasionally harrying settlements in the Nile Valley when the rains failed or food supplies ran low. Egyptian rulers periodically mounted raids to repel them and drive them into the desert; but they always crept back. Egypt's western neighbors were a persistent irritant, albeit a minor one.

The situation began to deteriorate at the end of the eighteenth dynasty. From the decoration in the Memphite tomb of Horemheb, we can see that campaigns involving Libyan foes evidently became more common during the reign of Tutankhamun. The battle reliefs of Seti I's reign, including those in the temple of Beit el-Wali, depict military action on Egypt's western borders. Two factors seem to have lain behind the upsurge in activity. First, a new tribal grouping, the Libu (who subsequently gave their name to the region as a whole), appeared. They were probably of Berber origin, perhaps from the southeast corner of present-day Libya. By the reign of Ramesses II, when they are first named in an Egyptian inscription, the Libu had displaced the Tjehenu and Tjemeh to become the dominant tribe along Egypt's Libyan frontier and the coast of Cyrenaica. Certainly the Libu seem to have been better equipped and better organized for military action than their predecessors, and hence posed a much more serious threat to Egypt's stability and territorial integrity. The second factor was the appearance of armed pirates off the Libyan coast, part of a more widespread phenomenon of population displacement and migration that seems to have affected much of the eastern Mediterranean in the thirteenth to eleventh centuries B.C. The names given to these piratical groups in Egyptian texts are various and exotic. The best attested are the Sherden, some of whom were captured during Ramesses' first taste of military action and subsequently incorporated as mercenaries into the Egyptian army. As we have seen, Sherden soldiers served as members of the king's personal bodyguard at the Battle of Kadesh. It was perhaps inevitable that the two groups – the Libu, with their detailed knowledge of the desert routes, and the Sherden, with their seafaring skills and coastal intelligence – would eventually make common cause and join forces to attack Egypt.

The seriousness of the threat can be gauged by the defensive response. Under Ramesses II, a series of major fortresses was built in a line from Memphis to the Mediterranean coast, guarding both the land and sea approaches to the western Delta.[15] They formed a counterpart to the twelfth-dynasty Walls of the Ruler in the eastern Delta but were a new departure for the region in question. To date, five forts have been identified by archaeologists: two on the western Delta fringes, at Tell Abqa'in and Kom el-Hisn, and three along the coast west of present-day Alexandria, at Gharbaniyat, el-Alamein, and Zawiyet Umm el-Rakham. (A later inscription from the reign of Ramesses III mentions three forts guarding Egypt's west coast, indicating that these three locations were maintained as military garrisons for several generations after their initial construction.) They were probably situated one day's march apart, a classic tactic for securing hostile territory. Moreover, each fort seems to have been built around a natural well or waterhole, which served to deny supplies of fresh water to any rebel force moving through the area: an inscription inside Zawiyet Umm el-Rakham refers to "fortresses [upon] the hill-country of Tjemeh and the wells within them."[16] The coastal forts originally stood some forty feet high and would have acted as landmarks for returning ships, as well as a deterrent against attack from the sea.

The best-known fort, excavated since 1994 by a team from the University of Liverpool, is the installation at Zawiyet Umm el-Rakham, some two hundred miles west of Alexandria.[17] It is a large construction, enclosing an area of nearly five acres and defended by mudbrick walls fifteen feet thick. The outer wall contained 1.6 million bricks, each of unusually large dimensions. A single gateway was flanked by two massive stone-clad towers, from which the Egyptian defenders could rain down missiles on attackers. All in all, the defenses were solid and impressive, clearly designed to withstand a concerted assault by a well-armed and determined enemy. Zawiyet Umm el-Rakham must have accommodated a large garrison, and some details of life inside the fort can be reconstructed from archaeological discoveries.

The religious life of the soldiers was well catered to at a limestone temple that was built against the interior western wall of the fortress facing east. Designed like a classic pharaonic temple in miniature, it had a main courtyard bisected by a paved processional way for use during religious processions. A pedestal served as a resting place for the divine image that priests would have carried in a portable shrine on such occasions. The temple area was provided with an elaborate system of drains and channels to remove standing water during heavy winter rains, and perhaps also to refill the fort's cisterns. In a clear illustration of Ramesside religious practice, the main temple, whose dedication remains uncertain, was accompanied by three smaller, crude chapels in the area immediately to the south. Each had a doorway facing east (toward the sunrise and Egypt); linking the three were a courtyard and small portico. The chapels seem to have accommodated one or more statue cults of Ramesses II. Even here, on the remote Libyan coast a good week's march from the edge of the Nile Delta, the pharaoh watched over his people, and his people worshipped him in return.

When they were not repelling attackers or offering prayers to their divine protector, the soldiers of Ramesses' western fortresses were kept busy providing assistance to the ships that plied the trade route between Crete and Egypt. Utilizing the winds and currents of the eastern Mediterranean, this route ran from the Nile Delta up the Levantine coast, along the southern coast of Anatolia, across the Aegean to Crete, and thence south to the coast of North Africa. Ships would have arrived in the vicinity of Zawiyet Umm el-Rakham before heading east along the coast to one of the mouths of the Nile, and then upstream to the port of Memphis. At various ports along the route they would have unloaded their wares and taken on new products to trade farther afield. A Bronze Age shipwreck discovered off Ulu Burun on the southwestern coast of Anatolia and tentatively dated to the reign of Seti I demonstrates the wide range of materials traded across the region in the thirteenth century B.C.: copper from Cyprus and tin from Anatolia, elephant ivory and ingots of blue glass from Syria, ostrich eggs from Nubia, amber from the Baltic, wine and olive oil from Canaan, and, of course, gold from the realm of the pharaohs. Inside Zawiyet Umm el-Rakham, nine mudbrick magazines provided storage space for such trade goods. Each unit had a limestone doorway, its jambs and lintels inscribed with the names and titles of Ramesses II to emphasize the royal ownership of the contents. The lintel above the entrance to the fifth magazine bore, in addition, a scene showing the commander of the fortress, a man named Nebra, worshipping the king's cartouches. Each storeroom measured fifty-two feet by thirteen feet and was provided with internal compartments for the convenient storage of different products. Abundant quantities of pottery were discovered still in situ: Canaanite amphorae, Cypriote base-ring juglets (perhaps used to store opioids), and Aegean stirrup jars (for olive oil). They provide direct evidence of Bronze Age trade, with goods from across the eastern Mediterranean arriving safely in Egyptian-controlled territory.

And not just goods but also the traders themselves: an unusual building inside the fortress consisting of three parallel chambers with a central standing stone each has been provisionally identified as a Canaanite temple. If this is accurate, the Egyptians, despite their official xenophobia (expressed in word and image in so many royal inscriptions), seem to have gone out of their way to make foreign merchants feel at home when operating on Egyptian soil. A Canaanite temple inside an Egyptian fortress on the Libyan coast would complement the abundant evidence of foreign cults at Per-Ramesses, and reinforce the picture of Ramesside Egypt as a thoroughly multicultural and multiethnic society. Indeed, on a block from the fort at el-Gharbaniyat, Ramesses himself is described as "beloved of Hauron," the Asiatic protector god.[18]

The presence of Canaanite merchants and cults in the far west of Egypt was a reminder that the country was inextricably a part of the wider Near East, a region of shifting allegiances in which the geopolitical situation remained sensitive and volatile. The Battle of Kadesh had not only failed to capture Kadesh or secure Amurru for Egypt; it had also resulted in the loss of Upe to the Hittites. Even the usually loyal petty rulers of Canaan were wavering in their allegiance to the pharaoh: in the years after Kadesh, the normal tribute was slow to arrive, and the restive Bedouins increased their attacks on Egyptian interests. Ramesses II's response was to mount a series of military campaigns in the Near East while carefully avoiding any further direct encounter with the Hittite army. Two years after Kadesh, perhaps to reestablish confidence and familiarity with the terrain, the Egyptian army undertook a brief expedition into largely friendly territory to the east of the Dead Sea.

The following season, branching out a little farther, the army campaigned through Galilee and into southern Syria. The aim of this action was the reconquest of the heavily fortified hilltop settlement of Dapur (probably Tell Sikkin Sarut) and of Tunip (Hamath-on-Orontes), strategic towns which had been captured by the great warrior pharaoh Thutmose III, but which had subsequently been lost to Egyptian control for 120 years. They stood now within the Hittite sphere of influence. The outcome of Ramesses' bold attempt was the capture of Dapur and the erection of a statue of the victorious pharaoh inside the town—a more tangible victory than the stalemate at Kadesh. However, the citizens of Dapur evidently rebelled as soon as his back was turned, and he was forced to mount a further mission two years later, this time traveling north up the Lebanese coast—a commemorative stela was carved at the river crossing of Nahr el-Kelb, north of Beirut—before striking inland for a return visit to Dapur. A commemorative inscription carved in Egypt after the event acknowledged (in passing) the necessity of a follow-up campaign, while (characteristically) lauding the king for a singular act of bravery:

As for this plan to stand and attack this town of the land of Hatti . . . His Majesty (life, prosperity, health!) actually did it twice in the presence of his infantry and chariotry. His Majesty (life, prosperity, health!) was at the front of his infantry and chariotry when he attacked the town belonging to the enemy of Hatti which is in the region of the town of Tunip in the land of Naharin. His Majesty (life, prosperity, health!) picked up his coat of mail to put it on [only] after he had spent two hours standing and attacking the town of the enemy of Hatti in front of his infantry and chariotry [without] a coat of mail on. Only then did His Majesty come and pick up his coat of mail to put it on. Now he had spent two hours attacking the town . . . without a coat of mail.[19]

The repetitious description of the king's act of valor (or foolhardiness) is reminiscent of the Poem, and very much in the approved style for such accounts.

In situ evidence for the Syrian activities of Ramesses II is provided by the occurrence of his name at the coastal sites of Tyre, Adlun, and Byblos, and by the discovery of three heavily worn stelae on either side of the Lebanon-Syria border. One was discovered in 1994 covering a Roman tomb at al-Kiswah, ten miles south of Damascus.[20] Made from local basalt, it is carved with a scene showing Ramesses accompanied by two male deities, probably Seth and Ra (identified, respectively, with the local Asiatic deities Baal and Shamash/El). The second stela was uncovered in 1999 in a mosque in the town of al-Turra, close to Jordan's northern border with Syria.[21] It, too, is made from local basalt, and a fragmentary inscription makes references to the Egyptian corn god Nepri and to "the bravest of soldiers," "rebels," and "their fortifications." An Egyptian attack on enemy towns to guarantee regular tribute seems to be indicated. The findspots of the two stelae indicate a route, confirmed by other Egyptian royal inscriptions, that ran inland from Egypt's northeastern border via Edom and Moab along the "King's Highway," then descended the high ground toward the northeastern shore of the Dead Sea before following the Jordan

Valley, traversing the territory to the east of the Sea of Galilee (an important part of the Egyptian province of Canaan), and finally running through the Hauran region north toward Damascus. A third stela was reported in 2008 from a site ten miles east of Damascus. Its inscription includes the name and titles of the "troop-commander and overseer of foreign lands, Seti," an individual known to have served as governor of Upe province under Ramesses II.

Taken together, all the evidence points to regular military activity having been undertaken in Syria-Palestine in the decade or so after the Battle of Kadesh, dwindling to tours of inspection in subsequent years, the latter largely confined to friendly territory. Yet despite erecting stelae throughout Egypt's northern empire, Ramesses failed to achieve his ultimate objective. The only Egyptian royal inscription found at Kadesh—and the northernmost pharaonic stela found to date anywhere in the Near East—was carved by Seti I. For Seti's son, the reassuring myth of Kadesh was preferable to the uncomfortable reality.

THE TRIUMPH OF DIPLOMACY

With no prospect of a decisive military victory by either side, the tense standoff between Egypt and Hatti dragged on for more than a decade after the inconclusive encounter at Kadesh. The Hittites had suffered serious losses on the battlefield, and as long as their control of Amurru was not threatened, they seemed content to let Ramesses play the warrior king, as he attempted to hold together his shaky coalition of Syrian vassal states. Besides, the Hittites had other concerns of greater strategic import. To the east of Amurru, beyond the Euphrates, lay the land of Hanigalbat, the remains of the once-mighty Kingdom of Mittani, which the Hittite Empire had displaced a half-century earlier as the leading power in the region. The ruler of Hanigalbat, Wasashatta, was an ally of the Hittites, and he had sent troops to Kadesh. In reality, Wasashatta's support was a form of "protection": it allowed Hanigalbat to maintain a semblance of independence without being absorbed entirely into the expanding Hittite realm. The problem for Wasashatta was that his rich lands were also coveted by an upstart new power in the region, the Kingdom of Assyria. Not long after the Battle of Kadesh, while Hatti and Hanigalbat were still licking their wounds, the king of Assyria, Adadnirari I, launched a sudden attack on Hanigalbat. Assyrian forces swept westward from their homeland in the Tigris basin, overcame Wasashatta's army, and installed themselves as his country's new overlords. It was a bitter blow for the Hittites, depriving them of a loyal client state and confronting them with a sworn enemy on the other side of the Euphrates. Adadnirari wrote to his Hittite counterpart demanding recognition as a "brother" and fellow "great king." Muwatalli was having none of it, as his scornful reply made abundantly clear: "You brag about Wasashatta and the Hurrian land. By force indeed you conquered. You have also vanquished my [ally] and become a 'great king.' But what do you keep saying about 'brotherhood'? . . . You and I, were we born of one and the same mother?"[22] With Assyria on the rise, the Kingdom of Hatti could ill afford another confrontation with Egypt.

Then, eleven years after the Battle of Kadesh, in 1263, the sixteenth year of Ramesses II's reign, a palace coup in Hattusa, the Hittite capital, shattered the diplomatic status quo across the Near East. Not long after Assyria's conquest of Hanigalbat, Muwatalli had died unexpectedly, to be succeeded as ruler of Hatti by his son Urhiteshup, who took the throne name Mursili III. The new king reigned over Hittite lands for about five years and then was deposed by his uncle Hattusili III. Hattusili, it may be remembered, had been installed as governor of Upe after Kadesh, and so had gained considerable experience of power politics in the febrile Levant. Perhaps he thought his nephew incapable of defending Hittite interests against the growing threat from Assyria. Regardless, Hattusili's coup plunged Hatti into turmoil and threatened to destabilize the wider region. Mursili was banished, first to Syria, then to Cyprus. But exile did not lessen his determination to regain his throne. He appealed to the Babylonians and, when they failed him, to the hated Assyrians for help. Neither power wished to pick a fight with Hatti, at least not over a dispute between royal relatives. Finally, in desperation, Mursili fled to Egypt, where his uncle's agents had no hope of reaching him. Incensed by this development, Hattusili sent a letter to Egypt demanding his nephew's extradition, but Ramesses II refused. Mursili's sudden arrival gave the pharaoh an unexpected bargaining chip in his long-running rivalry with the Hittites.

With no diplomatic resolution in sight, both sides began to ready for military confrontation. The Babylonians may have offered to cut their ties with Egypt (they had been on friendly terms since the marriage of a Babylonian princess to Amenhotep III) and send troops to bolster the Hittite forces. This in turn may have prompted Ramesses to march his own army into northern Canaan in the winter of his eighteenth regnal year: it was better to be prepared for an attack than to react when it arrived. An Egyptian commemorative stela set up at Beth Shan that same winter may have been connected with military maneuvers in anticipation of a spring offensive.

In fact, the confrontation never came. No sooner had the King of Babylon, Kadashman-Turgu, offered his assistance to the Hittites than he died. His successor had second thoughts about abandoning the country's long-standing friendship with Egypt: in such an unpredictable political climate, it might be wiser to stick with old allies. Hattusili found himself denied military support. And worse was to come. A new king in Assyria, Shalmaneser, was no respecter of diplomatic niceties. Sensing the Hittites' weakness, he swept his forces into Hanigalbat (which had gone back over to the Hittite side), deposed its puppet ruler, absorbed it into his own state, and wiped it from the map. In so doing, Shalmaneser brought an end to a proud royal line that had shaped the politics of the Levant for centuries. From his seat in Carchemish, the Hittite viceroy of Syria could now virtually look the enemy in the face on the other bank of the Euphrates.

Beset by enemies on every side, from his arch-foe to his own nephew, Hattusili seems to have decided that the only long-term solution lay in diplomacy. It is probable that he started to send out feelers to Egypt immediately following the Assyrian conquest of Hanigalbat, in Ramesses' nineteenth year on the throne. On the Egyptian side, Ramesses must have realized, despite his bluster and propaganda, that he would never win a pitched battle against the massed Hittite forces, never capture Kadesh. Egypt had more to gain in the long term from renewed access to Hittite-controlled ports such as Ugarit. A peace dividend would be Ramesses' freedom to indulge in his favorite pastime, building on a grand scale.

The end result, no doubt after delicate negotiations lasting many months, was a formal peace treaty between Hatti and Egypt.[23] Ratified in Ramesses' twenty-first year on the throne, 1259 B.C., it brought to an end some seven decades of conflict between the two powers. As might have been expected, the Egyptian account presented the turn of events as a victory: "The silver tablet which the great chief of Hatti, Hattusili, caused to be brought to Pharaoh (life, prosperity, health!) to beg peace from the majesty of the Dual King Usermaatra-setepenra, the son of Ra Ramesses-beloved-of-Amun, given life forever and ever."[24] Of course, neither side had won, but the treaty offered a new beginning. Preserved in two languages — a cuneiform version, on a clay tablet from the Hittite capital, Hattusa, and a hieroglyphic version, inscribed in stone on the walls of Karnak temple — the treaty is one of the most remarkable documents to survive from the ancient world.

The manner of its arrival in Egypt was no less extraordinary. According to the Egyptian text, the treaty arrived in Per-Ramesses on the twenty-first day of the third month of winter in the pharaonic calendar, equating to early November. It was brought from Hattusa — a month's journey by chariot — by six royal envoys. They must have timed their departure from the mountains of central Anatolia after the intense summer heat but before the first snows of winter. The names of the first three envoys are lost, but the second group presented a thoroughly multicultural picture. One bore the Hurrian name Tiliteshup and is known to have served as a Hittite royal envoy for at least fourteen years. He was evidently a career diplomat and is attested in the Hittite state archives at Hattusa as well as at Ugarit as a witness to a legal document between Hatti and one of its Levantine vassals. A second envoy, from Carchemish, bore the Hittite name Yapusili. Perhaps most interesting of all, the companion of Tiliteshup and Yapusili bore the Egyptian name Ramose (essentially a version of Ramesses). Like Tiliteshup, Ramose is attested elsewhere in Hittite diplomatic correspondence, and he also served for at least fourteen years. A native of the Nile Valley at a distant court, he must have been employed for his detailed knowledge of Egypt, its laws and customs.

The treaty itself followed a format common to Hittite diplomatic documents of the time. It was arranged in six sections. First came the title and preamble: "The treaty made by the great chief of Hatti, Hattusili the valiant, child of Mursili, great chief of Hatti, the valiant, grandchild of Suppiluliuma, great chief of Hatti, the valiant, upon a silver tablet; for Usermaatra-setepenra, the great ruler of Egypt, the valiant, child of Menmaatra, the great ruler of Egypt, the valiant, grandchild of Menpehtyra, great ruler of Egypt, the valiant: the good treaty of peace and brotherhood." It was normal practice for a Hittite king to proclaim his ancestry two generations back; the same formulation would doubtless have appealed to Ramesses, for whom membership of the Ramesside nineteenth dynasty was a source of particular pride.

Next came a historical prologue, setting out the arc of relations between Hatti and Egypt. The text did not shy away from mentioning the former hostilities, but emphasized the historic friendship that had existed between the countries, and looked forward to its resumption:

> Now at the beginning, since eternity, the relations of the great ruler of Egypt with the great chief of Hatti were such that the god prevented hostilities arising between them, by treaty. Whereas in the time of Muwatalli, the great chief of Hatti, my brother, he fought with [Ramesses], the great ruler of Egypt, yet afterward, beginning with this day, behold Hattusili, the great chief of Hatti, is in a treaty relationship for establishing the relations which Ra has made, and which Seth has made, for the land of Egypt, with the land of Hatti, in order not to allow hostilities to arise between them, forever.

The third section, forming the heart of the document, laid out the stipulations of the treaty. First and foremost was a mutual renunciation of any future hostilities between the two countries: "Behold, then, Hattusili, the great chief of Hatti, is in a treaty relationship with Usermaatra-setepenra, the great ruler of Egypt, in order to bring about peace and good brotherhood between us forever. . . . The grandchildren of the great chief of Hatti shall be in brotherhood and peace with the grandchildren of Ramesses-beloved-of-Amun, the great ruler of Egypt." Then came a reaffirmation of former treaties between Egypt and Hatti, which suggests that there had been two earlier diplomatic alliances, the first probably between Suppiluliuma and Amenhotep III or Akhenaten, the second perhaps between Muwatalli and Seti I. There is no evidence of either from the Egyptian side — but then, earlier pharaohs were keener to trumpet military victories than diplomatic compromises. The next stipulations are among the most interesting, and unprecedented, in the ancient world: a defensive alliance and nonaggression pact, and an agreement for the mutual extradition of illegal migrants and political fugitives. "If any great person flees from the land of Hatti and comes to Usermaatra-setepenra, the great ruler of Egypt, from either a town or a district belonging to the land of Hatti, and comes to Ramesses-beloved-of-Amun, the great ruler of Egypt, then Usermaatra-setepenra, the great ruler of Egypt, shall not receive them, but Ramesses-beloved-of-Amun, the great ruler of Egypt, shall cause them to be brought to the great chief of Hatti. They shall not [be allowed to] settle." This clause, no doubt, was included at Hattusili's insistence, to prevent any recurrence of the Mursili incident.

After the specific measures came a list of the divine witnesses: "As for the words, a thousand gods from the war gods and the female gods of those of the land of Hatti, and a thousand gods from the war gods and the female gods of those of the land of Egypt, they are with me as witnesses of these words." In addition, twenty-eight specific deities were invoked on the Hittite side, just three (Amun, Ra, and Seth) on the Egyptian side. The fifth and sixth sections would have been familiar to the Egyptians and Hittites alike: curses for any infringement of the treaty, blessings for adhering to it. The Egyptian translation ends with a precise description of the Hittite state seal that was stamped on both sides of the silver tablet.

The Egyptian-Hittite treaty succeeded in holding at bay Assyria's ambitions and ushered in a new era of friendship between two historic enemies. One immediate impact was the resumption of Egyptian trading activities at Ugarit: two presentation vessels bearing the name of Ramesses II have been found in the port, one in a private house, one in the ruler's palace. With Amurru and Upe now in friendly hands, the Egyptian province of Canaan no longer seemed so vulnerable. Settlements deemed no longer of strategic importance were abandoned, garrisons withdrawn. As for the two royal families at the heart of the diplomatic breakthrough, an extensive correspondence found in the Hittite capital suggests genuinely friendly relations.[25] Ramesses sent letters to Hattusili while Queen Puduhepa of Hatti corresponded with her counterpart in Egypt. In reply, the pharaoh's chief wife, Nefertari, assured her "sister": "May Ra and the Weather-God bring you joy, and may Ra ensure that it is a prosperous peace. He will make excellent the brotherhood between the Great King of Egypt and the Great King of Hatti, his brother, forever. And I am in friendship and sisterhood with my sister, the Great Queen of Hatti, now and forever."[26]

Ramesses also sent diplomatic gifts to the Hittite court, including gold vessels and jewelry, linen garments and bedding, furniture, and boxes inlaid with gold and lapis lazuli. In perhaps the most appreciated gesture of all, when members of the Hittite royal family fell ill Ramesses sent medicines and a skilled doctor. Egyptian medicine was famed throughout the ancient world, and the outcome of this particular medical assistance seems to have been successful, for Hattusili later requested a cure for his sister's sterility. Ramesses' reply, which offers a glimpse of his character, was both incredulous and exasperated: "As for Matanazi, my brother's sister . . . she is certainly sixty! No one can produce medicine to make her fertile. But of course, if Ra and the Weather God should wish it . . . I will send a good magician and an able physician and they will prepare some fertility drugs for her anyway."[27]

Perhaps the most remarkable outcome of the treaty was the arrival in the heart of Per-Ramesses itself of Hittite troops not as invading enemies but as welcome allies. For all his vainglory, Ramesses seems to have been a pragmatist. The military-industrial complex that housed the headquarters of his chariot divisions now played host to Hittite infantry. And the great bronze foundry that had produced the Egyptians' weapons for the Battle of Kadesh now turned out fittings for the Hittites' distinctive shields: a figure-of-eight design on one side, the stylized bull head of the Hittite weather god on the other.[28]

CHAPTER THREE

A New Colossus

Ramesses II's first instinct as pharaoh was to build. At the start of his reign – long before he launched his first military campaign to defend Egypt's interests and widen its borders – he ordered the completion of his father's unfinished monuments, the enhancement of existing temples, and the construction of new ones.[1] Indeed, the evidence suggests that the first three years of his reign were taken up almost exclusively with planning and initiating building projects in Egypt and Nubia. Part of his motive, doubtless, was to be seen to fulfill the age-old contract between the kings and deities of Egypt: each pharaoh was expected to beautify and maintain the gods' cult centers in exchange for divine blessings. The nineteenth dynasty, with its provincial, plebeian origins, seems to have been especially concerned to demonstrate its new royal credentials by carrying out the traditional duties of kingship.

But Ramesses' penchant for building went far beyond what might be expected of a king, even in the golden age of ancient Egypt's empire. His monumental ambitions were of a scale and scope unprecedented in the long sweep of pharaonic history, and unsurpassed afterward. Perhaps only Amenhotep III came close in the sheer number and size of buildings and statues commissioned by a single king. For Ramesses II, it was not only new commissions that preoccupied him: where he could not build anew, he carved his name on existing structures, to reappropriate them as his own. A modern tourist to Egypt quickly learns to identify the cartouches of Ramesses II, for they are carved more deeply (as much as two inches into the stone) than those of any other king before or since. Ramesses knew only too well that shallow inscriptions could easily be erased and recut—his workmen did just that on his behalf countless times. He seems to have been determined that *his* names would last for eternity and that no succeeding ruler would be able to efface or replace them. This must surely point to an aspect of his character: a determination to be seen by his own and succeeding ages as a great ruler, the greatest of all pharaohs.

The orgy of construction started as soon as Ramesses came to the throne. Beginning with the projects left unfinished by his father—the small temple at Beit el-Wali, the large memorial temples at Abydos and Qurna, and the great hypostyle hall at Karnak—he instituted an immediate change of style, from raised relief to sunk relief (quicker to execute and harder to efface), that signaled a deliberate change of policy. Quantity rather than quality, durability rather than finesse, seem to have been Ramesses' preoccupations from the start.

Abydos and Qurna were unmistakably Seti I's creations, and by completing them Ramesses was doing no more than a loyal son was expected to do. Karnak, however, presented Ramesses with a different opportunity: to recast an entire project as his own.[2] The Temple of Amun-Ra was a palimpsest in which the work of countless generations of Egyptian kings stood side by side, layer upon layer, in an accretion of architectural elements that together made up a vast complex of sacred buildings. The great hypostyle hall was no exception. The space it occupied, between the second and third pylon gateways of the temple, had first been delineated under Tutankhamun and Horemheb. Work on the hall of columns itself had begun under Ramesses I, the decoration of its exterior walls under Seti I. In completing the project, Ramesses II seized the chance to stamp his own mark so indelibly that the hypostyle hall would come to be regarded as one of his masterworks. It would henceforth be known by the resounding moniker "Glorious is Ramesses-beloved-of-Amun in the domain of Amun."

The main, defining feature of the hall was its forest of 134 sandstone columns, hewn from the cliffs of Gebel el-Silsila. One hundred and twenty-two of the columns, filling the two sides of the hall, were carved to resemble closed papyrus buds; each stood forty feet high. The central avenue lining the temple's processional axis was composed of 12 gigantic columns resembling open papyrus flowers, each nearly twice that height. The overall effect was stupendous, breathtaking. The hypostyle hall was a conscious re-creation of the primeval reed bed that, the Egyptians believed, had grown around the sides of the mound of creation when it first emerged from the waters of chaos at the beginning of time.

So much for high theology: Ramesses was equally invested in the decoration of the hall's exterior and interior walls, for these vast spaces offered the ideal canvas for representations of the king's military triumphs and cultic activities, respectively.[3] For a pharaoh whose self-image was intimately bound up with his martial prowess and pious works, the opportunity held great appeal. At Seti I's death, the northern half of the hall's interior had been fully decorated, largely with scenes of the king offering to the gods, and most of these were allowed to remain. Work had also started in the southern half of the hall, and here Ramesses began by continuing

Stamping his mark: In the great hypostyle hall of Karnak temple,
Ramesses' name occupies pride of place on every column (author photo).

the raised relief style of his father. But he quickly made the switch
to sunk relief, even re-carving the earlier sections in the new style
to avoid an abrupt change of aesthetic. The end result was to convey the impression, from the central axis of the hall, that the decoration of the hypostyle hall had been accomplished entirely by
Ramesses. It was a brilliant deception.

On the exterior walls, Seti I had begun the tradition of large-scale battle reliefs. Now Ramesses, to complement the Syrian campaigns of his father, depicted on the northern side, added scenes of the Battle of Kadesh on the southern side. Later, he had these covered with plaster and re-carved with scenes of his own (more successful) Syrian campaigns. The son seems to have been keen to emulate, equal, and indeed surpass his father's achievements.

To set a seal upon his work at Karnak, Ramesses completed the second pylon gateway, providing a fitting entrance to the hypostyle hall, and laid out an avenue of ram-headed sphinxes (the ram was sacred to the god Amun) stretching all the way from the pylon to the riverbank. Here a new stone quay enabled supply ships and ceremonial flotillas alike to dock in front of the temple, whence sacred provisions and cult statues could be carried in procession along the avenue, through the gateway, and into the heart of the temple via the splendor of the hypostyle hall. As a piece of theater, it was hard to beat. But according to Ramesses' designs, one final element was needed to complete the effect—one that would become his hallmark: a pair of colossal statues of himself, facing each other in front of the second pylon, guarding the entire religious complex. Was Karnak a temple to Amun or to Ramesses? The ambiguity was deliberate.

While the architecture with the greatest visual impact was reserved for the front of the temple facing the river, Ramesses did not neglect the rear of the complex, facing the local town. Here he completed the work begun by his father, and built a new chapel named "Amun who hears prayers." It enclosed within its sanctuary an obelisk erected by Thutmose IV in the eighteenth dynasty; Ramesses added a pair of new obelisks at the town entrance, fronting a monumental gateway.

The Temple of Amun-Ra at Karnak was the dominant structure of eastern Thebes, indeed the greatest religious building in the whole of Egypt, but it had an important satellite temple a couple of miles to the south, in the heart of present-day Luxor.[4] The "southern sanctuary" was ostensibly a place of divine recuperation which the god of Karnak could visit once a year during the Festival of the Sanctuary, to rest and recharge. More practically, Luxor Temple was designed to play a key role in the ideology of divine kingship, and it was used by both Horemheb and Ramesses II to legitimize their accession. The principal components of Luxor Temple dated to the late eighteenth dynasty: the sanctuary and solar court bore the imprint of Amenhotep III, while the processional colonnade had been begun by Tutankhamun and completed by Horemheb. It is possible that Seti I may have started work on a new forecourt. But it was Ramesses II who gave the building its present appearance, transforming its facade and turning the entire public face of the temple into a vehicle for his own glorification.

If one of his dedicatory texts is to be believed, he had been thinking about Luxor and how he might transform it since childhood. In a shrine to the goddess Mut (divine spouse of Amun-Ra), Ramesses claimed, "His Majesty (life, prosperity, health!) came to the throne thinking about her statue, and when he was a child, the heir apparent, he planned in his heart to rejuvenate her."[5] On the opposite wall of the temple forecourt, running around the inside, a longer inscription, dated to early in Ramesses' reign, recounts the king's decision to carry out work at Amun's southern sanctuary.[6] After extolling the king's qualities as a patron of religious buildings — "steeped in knowledge like Thoth, knowing how to instruct, skilled in craftsmanship" — the text goes on to boast that research carried out by the king himself led him to commission the work: "Now His Majesty searched the library, he read the books of the House of Life, and he learned the offering prescriptions of heaven and every secret of earth. He found that Thebes, the Eye of Ra, was a primeval mound . . . which had been in existence since the time when . . . Amun-Ra was king, illuminating the heaven. He divided its circuit, seeing a place where he might let his Eye alight: his right, Thebes, being the city of southern Heliopolis, and his left being Heka-anedj, the province of northern Heliopolis."[7] The "city of southern Heliopolis" was one of the common designations for Thebes, explicitly linking the southern religious capital with its more ancient, northern counterpart. In Ramesses' text, he took this comparison farther, insisting that Thebes had been selected as a place of divine favor at the dawn of creation. Such a pedigree fully justified his decision to build there.

In characteristic fashion, Ramesses then conveyed his decision to his assembled courtiers: "I have in mind to perform construction work . . . carrying out the work in his temple of the southern sanctuary." The rest of the fragmentary inscription describes details of the work: a flotilla of ships sailing south (presumably to the sandstone and granite quarries) with happy, healthy, and well-fed crews; troops lending a hand to carry out the work. The text is corroborated by indications from elsewhere in the Nile Valley of an extensive reconnoitering expedition to identify sources of building stone. At the end of his first regnal year, Ramesses paid a high-profile visit to Gebel el-Silsila and sent an expedition to the turquoise mines of southwestern Sinai. The following year he left an inscription on the island of Sai, a key military base in Upper Nubia, and a stela in the region of the First Nile Cataract, between Aswan and Philae. This last area was the source of fine granite for obelisks, statues, and architectural elements; in a later inscription, Ramesses told his stonemasons: "I went to Elephantine and examined a fine mountain so that I might give you the use of it."[8] Indeed, the king's self-proclaimed mastery over the natural resources of the known world was underscored in a procession of mineral-bearing regions which forms part of the decoration of the Luxor Temple forecourt. The anthropomorphized locations shown bringing their products to Ramesses range from the gold mines of Upper Nubia in the south to the islands of the Aegean in the north, from the Farafra and Bahariya Oases in the west to Babylon in the east.[9]

According to the Luxor dedicatory text, the entire construction project—comprising a new forecourt with a triple shrine and a monumental pylon gateway—was finished early in Ramesses' third regnal year, barely twenty-eight months after his accession to the throne. The king must have been pleased with the work, and the temple was given a new name to mark the occasion: "The temple of Ramesses-beloved-of-Amun united with eternity in the house of Amun." In the elegant reliefs inside the forecourt that accompany the dedicatory inscription (their refined style more reminiscent of the work of Seti I's reign), temple staff are shown carrying jars of beer for the daily offerings; the king is depicted offering to Amun-Ra and Maat (goddess of truth and righteousness), while his wife shakes sistra (sacred rattles) to appease Mut, and a row of young princes and princesses approaches a stylized representation of the new temple gateway, pennants fluttering in the breeze atop long flagpoles set into the niches of the facade. In these enchanting scenes, we perhaps catch sight of a new monarch, brimming with ambition and confidence, establishing his wider family as the new focus of the nation's attention.

By contrast, the new exterior, public facade foregrounded Ramesses himself. He usurped two colossal seated statues of Amenhotep III and had them set up in front of the pylon, flanking the entrance and looking along the processional route to Karnak. On either side of these colossi, he erected two massive obelisks, hewn from the granite quarries of the First Nile Cataract. (The earlier version of the king's throne name used on the obelisks shows that they were finished before the end of his second regnal year.) Some years later, the pylon's outer walls were covered with huge tableaux depicting the Battle of Kadesh. The point being made was unequivocal: under Ramesses, Luxor Temple was a temple to kingship, pure and simple.

NO STONE UNTURNED

One curious aspect of Ramesses' new additions at Luxor has intrigued generations of scholars: although it is not immediately obvious on the ground, a bird's-eye view of the building reveals that the forecourt and pylon are not aligned with the axis of the eighteenth-dynasty temple but are several degrees off. Ever since the Pyramid Age, the ancient Egyptians had been adept at setting out buildings accurately in relation to stars, natural landmarks, or other structures. Ramesses' architects could easily have followed the existing axis had they so chosen; the decision to do otherwise must therefore have been conscious and deliberate. A prosaic explanation is that a change of axis was necessary to avoid the riverbank; yet the modern course of the Nile, and probably the ancient course as well, lies some distance from the Luxor Temple forecourt. An alternative theory is that the new temple elements were oriented to be more accurately aligned with the southern extension of Karnak, two miles to the north. But the evidence for such a theory is tenuous. The third, and perhaps the most plausible, explanation is that the facade of Ramesses' new pylon was designed to create a straight line across the Nile to the site of his memorial temple on the west bank—just as Seti I had intended the hypostyle hall at Karnak to line up with his memorial temple at

Qurna. The key to Luxor may therefore lie in its counterpart on the opposite bank of the river: a colossal edifice named "The temple of millions of years of United-with-Thebes," but better known today as the Ramesseum.[10]

When the kings of the early eighteenth dynasty had chosen a remote desert wadi in the heart of the Theban hills, now the Valley of the Kings, as their royal necropolis, they were motivated by a desire to keep secret the location of the royal tombs. Experience had taught them that whatever their proscriptions or sanctions, a kingly burial always attracted unwanted attention from tomb robbers, within a short time of the tomb's being sealed. A tomb that advertised its presence far and wide – a pyramid, for example – presented an even greater target. The solution was to hide the royal sepulchers in a remote and inaccessible spot where the bodies of the dead kings might stand a chance of lying in peace for eternity. The difficulty with this approach was that in providing security it denied kings the other aspect of the afterlife they so earnestly desired: fame. A secret tomb was of little use in perpetuating a monarch's memory, still less his cult, post mortem. A compromise had therefore emerged, beginning in the reign of Thutmose I, whereby each hidden tomb in the Valley of the Kings was accompanied by a public place of worship on the low desert facing the town of Thebes. Each of these memorial temples provided the focus for a king's cult, both during his lifetime and after his death, and gave public expression to his achievements, earthly and cosmic.[11] Though resembling the temple of a deity, a memorial temple was dedicated to the ruler himself as an aspect of the Theban god Amun-Ra.

The memorial temples of the eighteenth dynasty ran in a line along the eastern edge of the Theban cliffs. Seti I had branched out, building his some distance to the north, near the modern town of Qurna. When Ramesses came to choose the location for his memorial temple, he selected a prominent site that was both directly across the river from the facade of Luxor Temple and close to the cultivation, making it more visible from the east bank. Foundation deposits discovered beneath the walls indicate that the project was begun early in Ramesses' reign, certainly before the end of his second regnal year, when work at Luxor would have been in full swing. The site marked out – a massive area covering nearly ten acres – forms a parallelogram rather than a rectangle, perhaps to avoid a preexisting structure with sacred significance. (Middle Kingdom tombs found under the temple include one that belonged to a magician.)

Unusually, we know the name of the architect of Ramesses' memorial temple: Penra. Using sandstone from the quarries of Gebel el-Silsila, he essentially followed the plan of Seti I's Qurna edifice, though (characteristically) on a larger scale. Building records indicate that five to seven sandstone blocks at a time, weighing some ten to nineteen tons in total, were transported in a single barge to the construction site.[12] Penra also incorporated features that were being introduced simultaneously across the river at Karnak, such as a gateway decorated with scenes of the king's triumphs and a hypostyle hall. The entire temple enclosure was surrounded by a massive mudbrick wall that on its eastern side joined the first pylon. This was provided with an internal staircase leading to the roof of the temple, which the royal astronomers and astrologers would have used for celestial observations. Sometime after the king's fifth year the sides of the pylon were, like their counterparts at Luxor, decorated with scenes of the Battle of Kadesh.

Inside the monumental gateway, the temple opened out into the first of two colonnaded courts. The pillars along the north side were adorned with statues of Ramesses in the guise of Osiris, god of the dead and lord of the underworld. This idea was copied from the nearby early eighteenth-dynasty memorial temple of Hatshepsut. Indeed, blocks from Hatshepsut's temple were found, re-carved, in the storerooms surrounding the Ramesseum, confirming that Penra and his colleagues took a keen interest in the buildings of earlier kings, and were eager to pick up ideas from the architects of the past. Another borrowing was the scene of Ramesses' "divine birth," modeled closely on those carved by Hatshepsut and Amenhotep III.

But the Ramesseum was an arena for innovation as well as tradition. The open space of the first court was dominated by a single seated statue of the living pharaoh. Known in Ramesses' own time as "Ra of the rulers," it measured some sixty feet high and weighed around a thousand tons. (And this was not the acme of Ramesses' megalomania: he may have had an even larger statue of himself, towering up to ninety feet high, erected at Per-Ramesses; four centuries after the king's death, it was cut up to provide convenient building material for a temple gateway.) The surviving fragments — the torso and elements of the base — later inspired Shelley's sonnet on the transience of earthly power, "Ozymandias." In Ramesses' day, the statue had its own chapel, and next to it stood a thirty-foot-high statue of the king's mother, Tuya, also with its own cult chapel: the Ramesseum was intended as a monument to an individual but also to a dynasty; in no other memorial temple was a queen mother given such prominence. A gateway on one side of the first court led to a small palace, complete with audience chamber, throne room, and balcony. This residence would have been used by Ramesses during his tours of inspection to the construction site, and perhaps also when he was visiting Thebes for major festivals. It further served to blur the distinction between the Ramesseum as a memorial temple and a venue for celebrating the living monarch.

A ramp from the first court led up to a second court, which was likewise decorated with Osirid statues of the king along the eastern and western sides, and dominated by not one but two colossal statues. The bust of one of these achieved nineteenth-century fame under the name of the "Younger Memnon" (see Chapter 5). Beyond the two courts, and reached via three shallow staircases, a hypostyle hall with forty-eight columns was laid out, lit by a clerestory. Like the second court, it was decorated with scenes of the king before the gods and of Ramesses' foreign campaigns, including the attack on Dapur. Farther back still lay a series of lesser halls, one of which sported an astronomical ceiling, another a relief showing the goddess of writing, Seshat, recording the length of Ramesses' reign (the "millions of years" of the temple's name) on the leaves of the sacred *ished* (persea) tree. This room may have served as the temple archive and scriptorium — the House of Life. A double shrine to the north of the hypostyle hall was dedicated to the two most important women in the king's life: his mother, Tuya, and his chief wife, Nefertari. Other rooms in the rear portion of the temple included a chamber that was open to the sky (perhaps for celestial observations), a small chapel to the sun god Ra, storerooms for temple furniture, areas for food preparation, and, at the back, a barque shrine for the cult image of the resident deity and the sanctuary.

Ramesses II's memorial temple was not just a monument to the living king and a center for the celebration of his eternal cult: it also played a major economic role for the city of Thebes and its hinterland. Surrounding the temple on three sides, but still within the mudbrick enclosure wall, stood a vast series of storerooms and barrel-vaulted granaries, with the capacity to hold enough grain to feed more than three thousand families (not far off the likely population of ancient Thebes) for a year. The supply of grain, especially in times of famine, was one of the most critical functions of any Egyptian government and underpinned the state's implicit contract with the populace. Grain was a precious commodity, so reserve stocks had to be kept somewhere secure. A high-walled, well-guarded, off-limits royal temple enclosure offered the perfect solution. The Ramesseum was also supplied with large amounts of wine, from up to seventy vineyards. Long after it ceased to function as a memorial temple, the complex continued to serve as an administrative center for the surrounding area.

Across Thebes and beyond, Egypt in the early years of Ramesses' reign reverberated with the sounds of stonemasons' chisels and the cries of foremen as work proceeded concurrently at locations the length and breadth of the Nile Valley. Scarcely any site of dynastic or religious significance escaped the attention of the king's architects and builders. In his first twenty years on the throne, Ramesses erected all the main buildings at his new Delta residence of Per-Ramesses, completed his father's cenotaph and built his own temple at Abydos, finished the great hypostyle hall at Karnak and the Luxor forecourt, began work on the Ramesseum, and built eight rock-cut shrines in Nubia, as well as undertaking projects at the northern- and southernmost extremities of his realm—a ceremonial gateway at Byblos on the Lebanese coast and a temple at Napata in Upper Nubia, close to the Fourth Nile Cataract. Maintaining such a frenzy of activity over such a vast distance offered an immense logistical and administrative challenge.

At some sites, Ramesses merely usurped the monuments of earlier rulers, adding his own names to claim ownership of temples and statues. But there were many locations where the king commissioned new cult buildings. He seems to have been determined to stamp his presence on the religious landscape of Egypt, just as he had left his mark on the physical landscape of the Near

East through the rock-cut stelae he left in prominent locations during his Asiatic campaigns. Ramesses' choice of sites for the foundation of new temples reveals something of his personal agenda. One such location was on the east bank of the Nile in Middle Egypt, just north of Akhenaten's capital city Akhetaten (present-day Amarna). Known today as Sheikh Ibada, the site was famous in classical times as Antinoöpolis, a city founded by the Roman emperor Hadrian in memory of his favorite, Antinous, who was said to have drowned in the Nile nearby. Hadrian enlarged a site that was already an established cult center, whereas it appears that Ramesses II chose a vacant location, building a temple where there had been none previously.[13] It was an impressive structure, with all the elements that characterize the temples of his reign: a massive pylon gateway leading to an open colonnaded forecourt, a hypostyle hall lit by a clerestory, and a sanctuary at the rear. The forecourt resembled the first court at the Ramesseum, with columns on each side and a portico with a double row of columns in front of the entrance. On the huge architraves, the king's names and titles were incised with carefully carved and painted hieroglyphs. Another point of similarity with the Ramesseum was the presence inside the court of a colossal statue. In this case, the object of veneration was a baboon (an animal sacred to the god Thoth, whose main cult center lay on the opposite bank of the Nile), originally painted with red fur and blue skin.

But the temple at Sheikh Ibada was not dedicated solely to Thoth. An interesting aspect of its decoration is the multiplicity of deities who were given prominence. On the external walls the king is shown offering to the chief state god and lord of Karnak, Amun-Ra. Inside the temple stand large cult statues to Sekhmet (lioness goddess of war and pestilence), Hathor (cow goddess, divine mother and protector of the king), and Horus (falcon god of sky and divine kingship). Many more gods are referenced in word and image on the columns – so many, in fact, that it has proved impossible to identify a principal deity to which the temple was dedicated. Rather, the temple seems to have celebrated all the gods, local and national, with Ramesses as their high priest. Indeed, from the central aisle of the temple the multiple images of the king on the columns, where he is shown presenting offerings to the gods and goddesses, are always visible. Ramesses' motive for commissioning a brand-new temple in a relatively remote, provincial backwater may have been to "cleanse" this stretch of the Nile Valley from the lingering taint of Akhenaten's revolution and reclaim the site for the traditional gods of Egypt – while at the same time claiming the credit for himself and emphasizing his role as defender of religious orthodoxy.

It is noteworthy that the temple at Sheikh Ibada is mostly built from small stone blocks, reused from nearby Akhetaten; some had to be covered with a thick layer of plaster to conceal earlier decoration. The last buildings left standing in Akhenaten's abandoned capital must have been dismantled for use in Ramesses' construction project. Although Akhenaten died four decades before Ramesses' accession, the memory of the heretic pharaoh still lingered, especially within the royal family. Horemheb, patron of the nineteenth dynasty, had begun his career under Akhenaten; his Memphite tomb, still the focus of reverence in Ramesses II's time, betrayed the influence of Akhenaten's artistic legacy. The artists who had decorated the royal tomb of Ramesses I had likewise been trained under Akhenaten. Now Ramesses I's grandson took the opportunity to erase the final vestiges of the heresy from art and architecture, and to airbrush the "time of rebellion" from history.[14] Ramesses II's temple to the traditional gods of Egypt at

Sheikh Ibada can be seen in this light: the final nail in Akhenaten's coffin and the vigorous proclamation of a return to the old ways.

At the core of the traditional Egyptian pantheon was the sun god Ra, worshipped since the beginning of Egyptian history as the creator of life. His principal temple, and the epicenter of his cult, lay near the junction of the Nile Valley and the Delta, in the place called by the ancient Egyptians Iunu (biblical On, classical Heliopolis). Countless generations of pharaohs had lavished attention on the Heliopolitan temple of Ra. Now Ramesses II determined, as part of his temple-building program, to beautify this most sacred and symbolic of buildings.[15] His research in the archives, quoted above, had revealed to him the special theological connection between Thebes ("southern Heliopolis") and its northern counterpart. So it was only natural that the great builder in the former location should soon turn his attention to the latter. Recent systematic excavations in the main temple enclosure at Heliopolis have revealed the extent of Ramesses' work. As at Sheikh Ibada, he made good use of the dismantled buildings from Akhenaten's reign. He also usurped much earlier, twelfth-dynasty statuary. In characteristic fashion, Ramesses added a hypostyle hall—this one with columns of red granite, a stone with strong solar connotations—and colossal statues of the gods and himself. One such, also of red granite, stood twenty feet high, dominating its courtyard. And Ramesses did not stop there. Along the central axis of the main temple he erected a second cult building, perhaps dedicated to the Theban divine couple Amun and Mut, and thus forming another symbolic link with his work at Luxor. Its facade was likewise adorned with colossi of the king, and the courtyards were filled with smaller divine and royal statues. South of the main axis, a third temple was commissioned by Ramesses. It may have guarded a processional route leading to an avenue of sphinxes and connecting the main temple gate with the obelisk erected by the twelfth-dynasty king Senusret I. This third sacred structure was decorated with reliefs showing Ramesses offering to two aspects of the sun god. Its facade sported the usual colossal statues, including the king in the form of a sphinx, carved from red granite.

Taken together, the temples completed or commissioned by Ramesses II at sites across Egypt can be seen as parts of an integrated, systematic plan. The king's goals seem to have been to rededicate and thus appropriate for himself every significant religious site in the country; to draw symbolic connections, through design and decoration, between disparate locations, weaving them together into a dense theological tapestry; and to usher in a new golden age of pharaonic religion, characterized by a bold new architectural style, eradicating all remaining traces of Akhenaten's heresy and proclaiming Ramesses as the model pharaoh. A new colossus indeed.

APOTHEOSIS

At Abydos, Ramesses proudly proclaimed himself his father's true heir. At Karnak, he was high priest of Amun; at Luxor and the Ramesseum, divine king; at Sheikh Ibada, high priest of all the gods; and at Heliopolis, son of the creator. None of these temples went so far as to make Ramesses himself, the living monarch, the explicit focus of its cult, even if the colossal statues set up at every opportunity were often worshipped in their own right. Egypt, after all, belonged to the traditional gods. There was barely a square inch of soil anywhere in the Nile Valley or Delta that was not already claimed by one deity or another. Not even the most self-aggrandizing of eighteenth-dynasty pharaohs, Amenhotep III, had dared take the ultimate step and erect a temple to his living self within the borders of his own country. Nubia, on the other hand — that stretch of conquered Nile Valley at once contiguous with, but politically and theologically separate from, Egypt — was a different matter. In the lightly inhabited territory between the First and Fourth Nile Cataracts, vast tracts of land lay unclaimed by any god: unclaimed, and thus ripe for royal appropriation.[16]

Amenhotep III had seized the opportunity, founding a temple to his deified self ("Amenhotep, Lord of Nubia") at Soleb. His son Akhenaten had followed suit at Sedeinga. None of the four succeeding pharaohs — Ay, Horemheb, Ramesses I, or Seti I — had taken the same bold step. But Ramesses II, in this respect at least, was happy to hark back to the late eighteenth-dynasty model of kingship. On his accession, he sent his surveyors and architects out to scout the Nubian low desert for suitable sites. Altogether, Ramesses founded at least seven new temples in Nubia, beginning with Beit el-Wali (the most northerly), constructed while he was still crown prince.[17] Aksha, near the Second Cataract, had been begun by Seti I; Ramesses completed it and dedicated it to "Ramesses the Great God, Lord of Nubia." Other early commissions included a new temple at Kubban, administrative center of the gold-mining region, and additions to the Temple of Amun-Ra at Napata. Alongside these small-scale projects, Ramesses also planned a more ambitious undertaking: a series of four new temples across Nubia, each dedicated to one of the four main state gods. At Derr, he would establish "The temple of Ramesses in the domain of Ra"; at Gerf Hussein, the shrine would be dedicated to Ptah; while at Wadi es-Sebua, Ramesses would establish a new cult center for Amun. But first and foremost, he intended to find a suitable site to dedicate to the most important member of the quartet: himself.

As early as the first year of his reign, his officials reported back that they had found the perfect spot.

The locality called Meha stood on the west bank of the Nile, just above the Second Cataract. There was a relatively rich agricultural zone on the opposite side of the river, which extended all the way to the northern end of the rapids. In consequence, this was one of the most populated parts of Lower Nubia. Meha itself seems to have been regarded as sacred from early in Egyptian history. It is not difficult to see why: dominating the spot was a vast cliff with a sheer face plunging down to a narrow plain above the water's edge. By Ramesses' day, the cliff face was littered with graffiti recording the visits of travelers and pilgrims during Egypt's Pyramid Age. More recently, Ay and Horemheb had excavated small rock-cut chapels into the nearby hills. Meha thus came with a good pedigree, but was as yet virgin territory.

Work on Ramesses II's grand design seems to have begun as soon as he came to the throne. The Nubian expedition in the second year of his reign may have been partly intended to gather prisoners of war to serve as a captive workforce; the man in charge of his commission, the royal agent Ashahebsed, recounted: "Now as for His Majesty (life, prosperity, health!), his mind was alert in seeking out every opportunity to perform good deeds for his father, Horus, Lord of Meha. . . . He carried off many laborers, captured by his strong arm from every foreign land." Construction commenced almost immediately, although such was the scale of Ramesses' ambition that the whole project would take more than three decades to complete. The site, known today as Abu Simbel, comprised two enormous temples, hewn into the living rock.[18]

The lesser of the two is known today as the Small Temple but this label belies its scale. The facade is carved to resemble a double pylon. At either side of the entrance a standing statue of the king's chief wife, Nefertari, is flanked by two statues of her husband, each within a massive rock-cut niche. The royal spouses are surrounded by statues of their children; these look diminutive alongside the thirty-foot-high colossi, yet they are almost life-size. Behind the facade, the temple is cut eighty feet into the cliff. Inscriptions on the frontage give a matter-of-fact (and rather repetitive) account of the thinking behind the project: "Usermaatra-setepenra, he made a monument by excavating in the mountain, as a work of eternity in Nubia. . . . His Majesty commanded the creation of a temple in Nubia by excavating in the mountain. Never was the like done before."[19] Inside, the first room is a six-pillared hall, decorated in a subtle white-and-gold color scheme with royal and divine figures. Ramesses is shown smiting the enemies of Egypt, watched by his wife. Next comes a vestibule, in which the royal pair is shown offering to Hathor, goddess of queenship and the western mountain, and protector of foreign lands. On the back wall of the sanctuary, at the rear of the temple, Hathor is shown again as a cow emerging from the marshes, with the king nestled under her head. Throughout the temple, the imagery deliberately associates Nefertari with Hathor, and this is reflected in its twin dedication to goddess and queen.

To the south of the Small Temple lies its bigger twin, and here the deification focuses squarely on Ramesses.[20] The Great Temple certainly lives up to its designation, extending some 160 feet into the cliff face. The unprecedented challenge of excavating, rather than building, an entire temple necessitated some adaptations to the classic Ramesside plan. The cliff face itself serves as the pylon gateway, and the entrance opens on to an eight-pillared hall, instead of the usual open court. Attached to each square pillar is a standing Osirid statue of the king (as at the Ramesseum), ten feet high. The ceiling is decorated with flying vultures and the king's cartouches, while reliefs along the north and south walls, carved in sunk relief with rich polychrome painting, depict his military victories in Syria, Libya, and Nubia. On the south wall his army storms an unnamed Syrian fortress, while the north wall is devoted to the Battle of Kadesh. These scenes of the famous encounter are unusual because they were signed by the man who carved them, the king's chief sculptor, Piay son of Khanefer. The back and front walls of the pillared hall show the king killing his enemies and presenting them to two pairs of deities: Amun and Mut on one side, Ra-Horakhty and an obscure goddess named Iusaas ("she is, and she is great") on the other. In both scenes, the seated image of the deified Ramesses was later inserted between the two deities, showing that the decision to feature the king's self-deification prominently in the decoration of all areas of the temple occurred at some point after the construction and decoration of the monument had begun. But there were no second thoughts: images of Ramesses the god take pride of place in the decoration of all the inner chambers.

Eight side rooms, possibly intended as storage for temple equipment, open off the main hall; each is decorated — rather crudely, by comparison with the principal rooms — with scenes showing the king making offerings to various deities. Beyond the eight-pillared first hall is a second hall of four pillars, equivalent to the second court of a classic temple. Originally two falcon-headed sphinxes flanked the connecting doorway. The decoration of the second hall, and of the vestibule which lies beyond, is purely religious, comprising scenes of the king presenting offerings to, or performing rites for, his deified self. These chambers thus act as a prelude to the sanctuary which lies at the back of the temple. On either side of the doorway leading to the holy of holies, a figure of the king with his arm extended is accompanied by an inscription which commands the priests, "Enter into the sanctuary, thrice purified!" The cultic heart of the temple is a simple, rather plain room, but its theological message packs a punch. Behind an altar in the middle of the room, cut into the living rock of the mountain, are four statues of the presiding deities of Ramesside Nubia, seated side by side. On the far left—permanently in the shadows, as befitted a god with chthonic associations—is Ptah, creator god of Memphis. Balancing him on the far right is the solar creator god of Heliopolis, Ra-Horakhty. Between these two, holding center stage, are the two most important deities of nineteenth-dynasty Egypt: Amun, lord of Karnak, and next to him the deified Ramesses II. No clearer indication could have been given of the primary dedication and purpose of the entire monument, whose ancient name was "The temple of Ramesses-beloved-of-Amun."

The exterior facade reinforces this association in dramatic fashion. It is dominated by a row of four enormous seated statues of the king, each more than seventy feet high, flanked by much smaller standing statues of his mother and chief wife, with diminutive statues of the royal children between their father's feet. Each of the king's colossi had its own name: "Ra of the Rulers" and "Ruler of the Two Lands" to the south of the temple entrance, "Beloved of Amun" and "Beloved of Atum" to the north.[21] Somewhat eerily, the eyes of the four statues are angled downward so that they appear to scrutinize anyone visiting the temple. At Luxor, the Ramesseum, Heliopolis, and elsewhere, massive statues of Ramesses II adorn the temple facade; at Abu Simbel, they *are* the temple facade. The distinction is significant. Everything about the Great Temple announces it as a cult center built by the king for the king and dedicated to Ramesses the god. Behind the four seated giants, the cliff face has been cut away to resemble a pylon gateway; it is topped by a cornice with a row of baboons facing east, their arms raised in adoration of the rising sun. In this instance, the rising sun is not the solar orb, but the king. This is made clear by the central element of the decorative scheme: a massive niche, directly over the entrance to the inner chambers, which contains a cryptographic writing of the pharaoh's throne name, Usermaatra, in which the god *Ra*-Horakhty is flanked by the goddess *Maat* and the scepter of power (*user*). In the depths of the sanctuary, Ramesses sits shoulder to shoulder with Amun, whose very name meant "the hidden one." But on the exterior, in full public view, facing the sun, Ramesses has become one with the solar creator. To underscore this association, the architects of the temple had one final trick: the entire monument was aligned in such a way that on two days of the year, February 20 and October 20, the rising sun penetrated all the way to the sanctuary to illuminate the figures of Ra-Horakhty, Amun, and the king. (In spring, the sun's rays would pass from Amun to Ramesses, in the autumn from Ra-Horakhty to the pharaoh; thus did the two gods transmit their divine radiance to the king, making him divine in turn.) Neither date is known to have been an important religious festival, but one of them is assumed to have been Ramesses' birthday. If so, the Great Temple at Abu Simbel must represent one of the most audacious examples of megalomania in the history of architecture.

It is the two temples, and especially the four giant colossi of Ramesses, that dominate the appearance of Abu Simbel today, just as they must have done in ancient times. But many additional elements appear in the sacred landscape, each of which serves to elaborate or intensify the central theological message. Running in front of the Great Temple is a terrace, its sides carved with row upon row of Asiatic and Nubian captives dominated by repeated royal cartouches: Ramesses the conquering hero. Along the terrace, stat-

Apotheosis: One of the four colossi of Ramesses forming the facade of the Great Temple at Abu Simbel; over the statue's right shoulder is a lifelike relief of the king, offering to his deified self (author photo).

ues of the living and resurrected king alternate with images of the celestial falcon: Ramesses the ever-living monarch, embodiment of the sky god. At the north end of the terrace is a chapel to Ra-Horakhty, at the south end a sanctuary to Thoth: sun and moon united in the person of the king. Farther south, a single rock-cut chamber served as a "birth house"; this was the shrine attached to a major temple in which the presiding deity's birth was celebrated. At Abu Simbel, as the orientation of the principal temple made clear, the birth in question was that of Ramesses himself.

Beyond ancient Meha, too, the king lavished unprecedented attention on Nubia, no doubt because it was largely virgin territory — Ramesses displayed a marked preference for sites that he could make entirely his own. To complement Beit el-Wali and Derr, he commissioned a partly rock-cut, partly free-standing temple at Gerf Hussein, which became the focus of construction during his fourth decade as king. It combined all his favorite elements that had been introduced at other sites: an avenue of ram-headed sphinxes leading from the Nile (as at Karnak), a peristyle forecourt decorated with Osirid statues (as at the Ramesseum), and a pillared hall and a sanctuary with four divine figures (as at Abu Simbel). Gerf Hussein was nominally dedicated to Ptah, but the cult statues in the sanctuary told a more nuanced story: they represented Ptah of Memphis, Ptah-Tatenen (the embodiment of the primeval mound of creation), Hathor, and — naturally — Ramesses.

Indeed, from the forty-second year of his reign on, Ramesses sometimes added the epithet "God, Ruler of Heliopolis" to his royal titles, identifying himself explicitly with the sun god and creator. He transformed a range of other Nubian sites, which showed evidence of earlier royal patronage, to reflect this self-image. Hence at Ellesiya, a rock-cut shrine built by Thutmose III, Ramesses restored the interior, re-carving the deities in the sanctuary's niche to represent Amun, Horus, and himself. At Wadi es-Sebua, a site first developed by Amenhotep III, Ramesses built the temple of "Ramesses-beloved-of-Amun in the domain of Amun," using prisoners of war taken during a raid on the Western Desert oases; in the sanctuary, Ramesses was depicted worshipping himself at the center of a divine family.

These projects, though impressive in their own right, were only ever intended as sideshows in a program with Abu Simbel as the star attraction. Throughout the middle decades of Ramesses' reign, the continued beautification of the temples at Meha seems to have remained his pet project. The surrounding cliffs bear the inscriptions of viceroys of Kush and other high officials, suggesting that an entire settlement grew up to service the sacred site. Even after construction was complete and the temple was formally dedicated, in the king's twenty-fourth regnal year, work continued on the decoration. But in his thirtieth year on the throne, a major earthquake struck Nubia, causing pillars inside the Great Temple to crack. The north doorjamb collapsed, and the seated colossus to the north of the main entrance lost an arm. Worse still, the entire upper body of colossus to the south of the entrance sheered off and landed on the ground in front of the temple. This must have been a devastating blow, especially for a monarch who from a young age had claimed to command the forces of nature: as crown prince, he had supposedly detected a previously unknown source of fine-quality granite at Aswan; this had been followed by further miracles, including finding water in the desert, and locating a massive block of quartzite "the like of which had never been found since the beginning of time." (He duly had it carved into a statue of himself, sixty-seven feet high, to adorn Per-Ramesses; it was named "Ramesses the God.")[22] But even the omnipotent pharaoh was powerless against an earthquake. When reports of the damage reached him, it was already too late; all he could do was order remedial work. The internal pillars were shored up, the cracks plastered over, the arm of the northern colossus reattached. But the southern colossus was beyond repair. Its fractured torso and head still lie at its feet, a lasting monument not to apotheosis but to hubris.

GOD AND KING

Inside the first pillared court of the Great Temple at Abu Simbel is a large stela dated to Ramesses' thirty-fifth regnal year which was probably installed to commemorate the conclusion of building and repair works at the site. It may even have been composed as an attempt to interpret the earthquake in positive terms, as a good omen from a chthonic deity.[23] The stela bears an extensive inscription in which the god Ptah promises the pharaoh millions of jubilees and all the other perquisites of Egyptian kingship, while Ramesses, in reply, boasts of his piety toward Ptah and his fulfillment of the contract between an Egyptian ruler and the gods. Known as the "Blessing of Ptah," the text was evidently so important to Ramesses as an affirmation of his reign that he had copies set up at two other temples in Nubia, Aksha and Amara West, as well as at Karnak. The inscription includes some important historical references, such as the foundation of Per-Ramesses – "You have made a noble Residence, to fortify the border of the Two Lands – 'The House of Ramesses-beloved-of-Amun, given life' – that it may flourish on earth like the pillars of heaven" – but it is primarily a theological text.[24] Nonetheless, it provides a window into Ramesses' world, because of the aspects of his rule and his relationship with the gods that it chooses to emphasize.

Appropriately enough for an inscription carved inside the greatest rock-cut temple of all, one of Ptah's gifts to the king is mastery of the natural world. In words that repeat one of the leitmotifs of Ramesses' reign, the god declares, "I cause the mountains to fashion for you great, mighty, perfect monuments. I cause the hill countries to create for you every noble precious stone to use for monuments in your name." The focus of Ramesses' pious deeds for Ptah, as recorded in the inscription, is not in Nubia, however, but in the god's principal cult center, far to the north, at Memphis.[25] Since the foundation of the Egyptian nation-state, at the beginning of the first dynasty, the so-called Balance of the Two Lands, where the Nile Valley and Delta meet, had been the location of the country's administrative capital. Here royal accessions, coronations, and jubilees were proclaimed, and the government bureaucracy was headquartered. One of the earliest monumental buildings ever erected in Egypt was the royal citadel at the heart of the city. Known as White Walls, its whitewashed, paneled, and buttressed mudbrick enclosure wall became an icon of kingship and a symbol of the rule of divine kings over the land of Egypt. From the first dynasty, too, the god most closely associated with Memphis was Ptah. (The very name "Egypt" derives, via the Greek *Aegyptos*, from the ancient Egyptian *Hikuptah*, "The temple of the spirit of Ptah," a moniker originally applied only to Memphis, but later to the country of which it was the capital.) Ptah was a chthonic god in origin, but he took on a bewildering array of attributes over the succeeding centuries. He was particularly closely associated with craftsmen, and in his own act of divine craftsmanship was believed to have created the world. According to another theological text, Ptah brought the universe into being through divine utterance. More prosaically, Ptah was a god "who hears prayers" and to whom ordinary Egyptians addressed their petitions. This aspect of Ptah's nature was particularly emphasized in the nineteenth dynasty, when it seems to have suited Ramesses to promote popular religion accessible to the masses alongside his own deification.

Throughout Ramesses' reign, while Per-Ramesses was the royal residence and Thebes the preeminent ceremonial city, Memphis remained the seat of government. It was here, therefore, that the potential tension between god and king—between divine monarch and head of state—was most acutely felt. The same person who handed down orders to his vizier and high officials in the audience chamber of the royal palace was the focus of worship a few streets away, both inside and outside the temple of Ptah. The Ramesside remains at Memphis and its principal necropolis of Saqqara provide a vivid illustration of the complex, dual nature of Egyptian monarchy.

Until recently, the sacred buildings of ancient Memphis lay largely undiscovered, covered by palm plantations, fields, and the accumulated sand of millennia. The best-known pharaonic monument visible at the site today is an immense colossus of Ramesses II, lying on its back since antiquity, too heavy even for modern machinery to lift back into place.[26] It is one of many such statues that were set up in front of major temples throughout the land to proclaim the king's divinity. Cult statues erected inside every temple sanctuary likewise depicted the pharaoh, either alone or shoulder to shoulder with the presiding deity. In many of the surviving examples of these statue pairs, Ramesses is better carved and larger in scale than his divine companion, so that he dominates the composition. Indeed, in many cases, the accompanying god is even named after the king — for example, "Amun of Ramesses" at Karnak and "Ptah of Ramesses" at Memphis — clearly indicating that the king was the senior partner.[27]

That Ramesses made spectacular additions to the sacred precinct at the heart of Memphis is confirmed by the "Blessing of Ptah":

> I have enlarged your temple at Hikuptah, protected with everlasting works, with effective labor, in stone, adorned with gold and genuine precious stones. I built your northern court, adorned with a noble double entrance before you. Their two doors are like the horizon of heaven, causing strangers to worship you. I made a noble temple for

you inside the enclosure. O God, whom I have fashioned, you are in its secret carrying shrine, resting upon its great throne. It is equipped with pure priests, divine servants, slaves, lands, and cattle. It is made festive with countless divine offerings consisting of all things.[28]

The text confirms an earlier inscription which indicates that Memphis was a focus of royal benefactions from the start: "Year 3, first month of winter, day 4. . . . Now His Majesty was in Hikuptah, performing praises for his fathers, all the gods of Upper Egypt and Lower Egypt, that they might grant him valor and victory, and a great lifetime of millions of years."[29]

Thanks to ongoing excavations among the ruins of ancient Memphis, something of Ramesses' work can now be reconstructed. The temple enclosure of Ptah covered an area similar to that of Karnak; it must have ranked as one of the greatest religious complexes of the ancient world.[30] In front of the pylon and all along the axial gateways of the temple Ramesses erected colossal statues of alabaster, limestone, and granite; single statues, dyads, and triads; statues of Ptah, of sphinxes, of himself. One of these can be dated to his first two years on the throne; most of the others were commissioned later. In commemoration of a jubilee, sometime after his thirtieth regnal year, Ramesses added a hypostyle hall to the temple of Ptah, mirroring his addition to the temple of Amun-Ra at Karnak at the start of his reign. He also built a jubilee hall, a counterpart to the one at Per-Ramesses, its white limestone walls covered with brightly colored reliefs and texts showing personified localities throughout his realm presenting offerings, and at least two small temples — one dedicated to Ptah, the other to Hathor — outside the main enclosure, in another part of the city.

More intriguing is the discovery of a temple built some distance to the north, beyond the far shore of Lake Abusir, which once formed an important part of the topography of ancient Memphis.[31] All the familiar Ramesside elements are present: a pylon gateway leading to a forecourt, a hypostyle hall, and a sanctuary at the rear, elevated above the rest of the temple. The walls were built from high-quality limestone, reused from nearby tombs and pyramid complexes, while the temple itself was partially built on top of Pyramid Age sepulchers. Its location, too, harked back to the past, being at the beginning of the ancient processional route from Lake Abusir to the fifth-dynasty royal necropolis, with its pyramids and sun temples. Ramesses and his builders cannot have been insensible of the vestiges of earlier epochs all around: a conscious decision to recycle earlier monuments in the construction of a new one is likely to have been inspired by the pharaoh's interest in the past and his determination to draw an explicit link between his own reign and those of the great kings of yore. Surviving fragments of decoration from Ramesses' Abusir temple suggest that it was connected with royal rituals known to have been celebrated at Memphis in the days of Egypt's earliest rulers — especially the ritual run around sacred markers that demonstrated the king's continued fitness to rule. Other elements of the decorative scheme gave prominence to deities specifically associated with royal authority and legitimacy from the earliest times, such as Ra, Horus, and Nekhbet, the city goddess of Nekheb and tutelary goddess of Upper Egypt, one of the "Two Ladies" who confer on the king dominion over the Two Lands (Upper and Lower Egypt). At Abusir, as at Abydos — another location closely identified with the tombs of early kings — Ramesses' favored modus operandi was to express his political and ideological goals through monumental architecture.

Up on the plateau above Memphis, tombs of all ages jostled for position. Dominating the skyline were the pyramids of third-, fifth-, and sixth-dynasty kings. Surrounding them on all sides were the tombs of high officials, members of the administration who had lived and worked in the royal citadel of Memphis, and who chose to be buried — or, in most cases, were granted the privilege of a burial — overlooking the city that had given them wealth and status. From the beginning of the first dynasty to the end of the Pyramid Age, the most senior officials in the central government were buried in the Memphite necropolis. The eighteenth dynasty, with its Theban roots, had moved the country's center of gravity south; and it was in the Theban hills that the great panjandrums of the time had built their final resting places. But with the advent of the nineteenth dynasty, the pendulum swung back in favor of Memphis. Only officials with a close connection to Thebes — the southern vizier, the viceroy of Kush, the high priest of Amun, and other senior roles at Karnak temple — continued to be buried in its necropolis.[32]

The Ramesside private tombs of Memphis, long neglected by archaeology but now reemerging into the spotlight of scientific inquiry, paint an informative picture of the composition — and priorities — of government in the reign of Ramesses II. To date, over thirty tombs of the period have been excavated.[33] Although some are very large, commensurate with the status of their owners, the general standard of workmanship is poor compared with the private mortuary chapels of the eighteenth dynasty at Thebes. This general decline in standards mirrors what is seen in the royal monuments, where size and quantity seem to have been more prized than subtlety or quality. On the other hand, the private tombs of Ramesses' reign display many innovative features in their form (modeled on temples) and decoration (where religious scenes predominate, registers wrap around walls, and statues of deities often feature in the shrine).

A favored spot for tombs was the area surrounding the Memphite tomb of Horemheb. Leading members of the court who built their sepulchers nearby included the vizier Neferrenpet, and the king's own sister, Tia, who claimed a prize plot right next to Horemheb's monument.[34] Nonetheless, her burial exhibited decidedly shoddy workmanship: the walls were hollow, filled with rubble and chippings, while defective areas of stonework were plastered over. It seems to have been another Ramesside example of style over substance. The most interesting details are to be found in the decoration of the tomb chapel: offering bearers bringing a calf and a young oryx, and two horses (riding was a favorite pastime of the Ramesside royal family) in a specially constructed stable on board their own funerary barge. Behind the offering room was a small stone pyramid, a nod to the royal monuments of old standing proudly on the horizon.

Elsewhere in the necropolis, clusters of private tombs were erected by successive generations of prominent court families. Paser, for example, was a royal scribe and steward of the temple of Amun. His eldest son, Tjuneroy, rose even higher, serving as overseer of works on all the monuments of the Lord of the Two Lands, overseer of works on all the monuments of the king, chief controller of all the monuments of the king, chief lector-priest, *sem*-priest of the king, festival leader of all the gods, royal scribe, chief scribe, and overseer of the granary. These multiple offices would have taken him on official duties throughout Egypt, and given him particularly close access to the king. Tjuneroy's younger brother, Paser Junior, entered the same line of work, but never rose beyond overseer of builders. Next to Paser's tomb, and tacked onto its southern side, one of the smallest nineteenth-dynasty private chapels was built for a musician named Raia. He served as chief of singers of the cult of Ptah-Lord-of-Truth. In the decoration of his tomb, Raia is shown as a blind harpist, playing before statues of

Ptah and Hathor—perhaps in the very temples built at Memphis by Ramesses II.

The varied cast of characters attested in the Memphite necropolis also includes Khay, "gold washer of the Lord of the Two Lands," whose chapel includes a scene of gold refining; Pabes, a trader, who chose a scene of ships being unloaded at the dockyards of Memphis; and Iurudef, who officiated at the funeral rituals of Tia and her husband (also named Tia) and chose to be buried inside their tomb enclosure. At the bottom of the cliff, closer to the city of Memphis, other officials built their final resting places. These included a senior chariotry officer, Nakhtmin, who proudly bore the titles "first charioteer of His Majesty," "royal envoy to all foreign lands," and "overseer of horses." He was interred alongside his wife, who served as a chanter in a local shrine. The skeletal remains from the tomb comprised a man in his fifties, a woman in her forties, and their pet dog.[35]

Such individuals give a snapshot of the different ranks of the central administration under Ramesses II. In other parts of Egypt, too, opportunities existed for men of talent and ambition to rise through the ranks and achieve high office. One such, attested in an inscription at Abu Simbel, was Ashahebsed. He began his career in the army, as a commandant of troops under Seti I, before becoming a royal envoy and then a cup bearer at the start of the next reign. Here we see a familiar pattern in Ramesside Egypt: a military dynasty promoting men from the ranks into civilian office. Ashahebsed also succeeded, no doubt, because he read his new master well: his name, probably adopted at the start of Ramesses' reign to honor the new pharaoh, means "rich in jubilees." Another of Ramesses' appointees was Ameneminet, whose career moved back and forth between civilian and military duties. He began as a personal companion (childhood friend) to Prince Ramesses before being promoted to royal charioteer and superintendent of horses, then foreign envoy after the Battle of Kadesh.

Outside Memphis and Thebes, the best attested group of officials from the reign of Ramesses II are the viceroys of Kush. During the course of the king's six decades on the throne, no fewer than nine individuals are known to have held the position. The longest serving (from any period) was Setau, who was responsible for overseeing the construction of the king's later Nubian temples. Setau often presented himself in quasi-regal terms, perhaps compensating for Ramesses' elevation in Nubia to divine status. Taking a leaf out of his master's book, the viceroy left over a hundred inscriptions throughout the Nile Valley which chart his career and give a flavor of life in the corridors of power under Ramesses II:

> A ward of the palace, I grew up in the king's house. . . . I was noticed as a youth and appointed chief scribe of the vizier; I taxed the entire land with a great scroll. . . . His Majesty . . . [subsequently] appointed me high steward of Amun-Ra, king of the gods. . . . I was overseer of the treasury and festival leader of Amun. . . . Again my lord recognized my reputation . . . and I was appointed viceroy in this land, directing for him serfs in thousands and tens of thousands, and Nubians in hundreds of thousands. . . . I rebuilt all the temples of this land of Kush that had previously gone to ruin; they were renewed in the great name of His Majesty.[36]

From first to last, as divine monarch or head of state, Ramesses' preoccupation with building extravagant monuments was the constant theme of his reign.

CHAPTER FOUR

Sons and Lovers

W hen recalling his appointment as Seti I's co-regent, Ramesses chose to focus on the three key actions that sig-
nified his formal elevation from heir apparent to joint ruler: his
coronation ("He summoned the chamberlains to fix the regalia on
my brow"); the setting up of his own household ("He established
me with private apartments"); and the establishment of his own
harem ("He selected women for me").[1] The choice is telling. Coronation was a sacred rite that transformed a mere mortal into a
quasi-divine ruler. The term used in ancient Egyptian is the same
as the word for the sun's appearance at dawn. By this analogy, a
ruler's crowning and his formal investiture with the regalia of royalty marked his first appearance as a transcendent, eternal being.
It was the moment of supreme theological transformation in the
life of a monarch. The establishment of a household, by contrast,
was a commonplace marker of societal recognition: the moment
in any ancient Egyptian man's life when he left his parents' house
to be recognized by his community as an independent adult, at the
head of his own family. By focusing on these two actions, corona-

tion and setting up a household, Ramesses was pointing to the divine and mortal aspects of Egyptian monarchy. The third signifier of the prince's elevation, the establishment of his own harem, was neither an integral part of the rites of coronation nor a recognized rite of passage for an Egyptian male. Rather, its inclusion in Ramesses' account seems to point to personal preference. Being set up with his own bevy of concubines was evidently one of the most significant events of the young Ramesses' life.

The evidence from his reign certainly suggests that he gloried in his role as husband (to multiple wives) and father (to countless children). There is likely to have been a strong dynastic element in this: Ramesses would have been conscious that the nineteenth dynasty had come to power solely because its founder, Horemheb, had produced no heir of his own, and that the subsequent succession from Ramesses I to his son and grandson could so easily have been disrupted, and the dynasty extinguished, if the line had failed. Ramesses II, with a powerful sense of dynastic destiny, was clearly determined to ensure that his own royal line would continue under all circumstances. Taking multiple wives was also a long-standing habit of the Egyptian male elite, especially the country's rulers. In the eighteenth dynasty, kings had secured the allegiance of friends and rivals alike, both within and beyond Egypt, through carefully chosen marriage alliances. Yet, alongside the dynastic and diplomatic dimensions of royal marriage, the attention lavished by Ramesses on his chief wives suggests a genuine fondness. In this aspect of his reign, hinted at from the beginning, we may perhaps glimpse something of his true character and personality.

Among the many consorts taken by Ramesses during his long reign, two principal queens dominate the surviving record. Their offspring took precedence over those of lesser wives, and they were duly celebrated in the king's monuments and inscriptions. Both bore Ramesses children while he was still co-regent, so both marriages must have been solemnized before he became sole king. The first of these queens is *the* dominant female figure of Ramesses' reign. Her name, Nefertari, means simply "beautiful companion." It masks her origins, about which next to nothing is known. Unlike his role model Amenhotep III — who had garlanded his chief wife's family with honors, promoting them in order to further elevate his queen — Ramesses placed all his attention on Nefertari herself. Her role as *his* queen, not her own family background, was evidently what mattered. (One of her more unusual epithets was "good mother.")[2] A small item found in her tomb, a faience knob bearing the cartouche of King Ay, may hint at a family connection with Tutankhamun's immediate successor. It is conceivable that Nefertari may have been a granddaughter of Ay's, in which case she would also have been related by marriage to Horemheb's chief wife, Mutnodjmet, who was probably Ay's daughter. Such a connection would also, perhaps, have made Nefertari the last surviving descendant of the extended eighteenth-dynasty royal family. (The pink complexion given to Nefertari's images in the decoration of her tomb is reminiscent of the skin tone of the famous bust of Nefertiti, wife of Akhenaten.) Ramesses' marriage to such an heiress would have been a neat political move, though not something he would have wished to boast about, given the taint of heresy that attached to Ay as father-in-law of Akhenaten. Certainly, nowhere on the surviving monuments does Nefertari claim royal ancestry; perhaps her origins really were obscure, provincial, and best left unrecorded.

Where Ramesses did follow the example of Amenhotep III was in raising his chief wife to prominence in the great temples of the realm. Amenhotep had built his consort her own temple in Nubia, in which her elevation to godlike status matched his own. Ramesses

Immortal couple: Statues of Ramesses flank those of his first great wife, Nefertari (*second and fifth from left*), on the facade of the Small Temple at Abu Simbel (author photo).

did not go quite that far: the Small Temple at Abu Simbel, while superficially dedicated to Nefertari as a manifestation of the goddess Hathor, is more of a monument to the deified Ramesses. Nonetheless, the inscriptions on the temple facade do explicitly reference the king's chief wife, in terms every bit as glowing as those reserved by Amenhotep III for his queen: "The great and mighty monument for the king's great wife Nefertari-beloved-of-Mut, for whom the sun shines, given life."[3] Two aspects of this dedication are noteworthy. First, just as Ramesses took—early in his reign—the additional epithet "beloved of Amun," incorporating it into his cartouche as part of his birth name, so Nefertari took the corresponding phrase "beloved of Mut," likewise included within her cartouche. In this way, the royal couple became the embodiment on earth of the supreme divine pair, Amun of Karnak and his consort Mut (whose name means, simply, "mother"). Second, the phrase "for whom the sun shines" is not mere flattery. At Abu Simbel, as the orientation and iconography of the Great Temple make clear, Ramesses *is* the sun. So his compliment to Nefertari also includes, rather tellingly, a reference to his own deification.

Yet in ancient Egypt, even the love of a divine king did not guarantee a long life. In what must have been a bitter irony, Nefertari seems to have died shortly after the official dedication of the Abu Simbel temples. She is mentioned in inscriptions from that year (the king's twenty-fourth on the throne), but not on texts dating to his thirtieth year. She had, however, fulfilled her role as Mut to Ramesses' Amun in more than one way: not only had she been his chief consort, she had also borne him at least two sons and five daughters. Ramesses' grief at her passing, reflected in the magnificent sepulcher he created for her in the Valley of the Queens (discussed below), must therefore have been tempered by the fact that she had secured the royal line.

Ramesses would also have been consoled by the presence of a second wife, a woman who remained in the shadows, with no official role or status, during Nefertari's lifetime, but who subsequently came to prominence as the king's new chief consort. Isetnofret ("beautiful Isis") probably married Ramesses about the same time as Nefertari, during the reign of Seti I. Her background, too, is obscure, her origins unknown. Tentative, circumstantial evidence may point to a connection with Horemheb — if so, Ramesses' first two wives might have been chosen deliberately as the descendants of the last two pre-Ramesside pharaohs — but this remains hypothetical.[4] Although Isetnofret was given little or no public attention until after Nefertari's death, her position and esteem at court are demonstrated by the fact that the children she bore the king ranked alongside the offspring of the senior queen. Nefertari gave birth to his first son, Isetnofret to his second son and his first daughter. In fact, it would be a son of Isetnofret, not of Nefertari, who would eventually succeed Ramesses on the throne of Egypt. And it is on monuments of her sons, rather than those of her husband, that Isetnofret attains the most prominence. One of these describes her as "she who fills the columned hall with the scent of her perfume; her fragrance is like [that of] Punt [a fabled land of incense, probably modern coastal Sudan] . . . her beauty pervades the audience chamber and her fragrance the columned hall."[5]

Isetnofret and Nefertari were contemporaries, but the former outlived the latter by about a decade, dying probably around the thirty-fourth year of Ramesses' reign. The king then turned to royal precedent and his daughters to fill the important ceremonial and theological role of king's great wife. The first in line was his eldest daughter, Bintanat, who seems to have succeeded her mother, Isetnofret, while also sharing official duties with her half-sister, Meritamun. They would be followed in due course by Ramesses' fifth daughter, Nebettawy, and seventh daughter, Henuttawy.[6] But even in the rarefied, tradition-soaked pharaonic court, daughters acting as great royal wives for the sake of protocol were no substitute for a genuine consort — not, at least, for Ramesses. No sooner had Isetnofret disappeared from view than the king was contracting another marriage, one even more clearly freighted with political significance than his first two matches.

A remarkable archive of diplomatic correspondence found in the ruins of the Hittite capital, Hattusa (present-day Boghazkoy, Turkey), reveals that at the time of Isetnofret's demise, Ramesses was engaging in delicate negotiations with his Hittite counterpart, Hattusili.[7] Over many months, royal envoys traveled back and forth the eight hundred miles between Hattusa and Per-Ramesses, bearing letters and replies. The subject of the negotiations was the ultimate statement of the new entente cordiale between Hatti and Egypt: the marriage of Hattusili's eldest daughter to Ramesses.[8] The ruler of Hatti promised the pharaoh not just a royal bride but also a dowry to match, asking Ramesses to send an envoy to meet the princess and her train at the Hittite border post of Aya in southern Syria. The king of Egypt, flattered by this show of friendship from an erstwhile enemy, lost no time in making the necessary preparations. The governor of the Egyptian province of Upe, which bordered Hittite-controlled territory, was put on standby to receive the dowry, while the governor of Canaan was instructed to escort the bridal party safely through the Levant to the Egyptian border. But then, as everything looked to be in place, a delay ensued— probably occasioned by Hattusili's having to leave Hattusa to deal with problems elsewhere in his extensive realm. Keen to conclude the match, Ramesses wrote, somewhat testily, to the Hittite queen, Puduhepa, who seems to have been put in charge of the negotiations in her husband's absence, urging a swift resolution. The contents of Ramesses' letter, referenced in Puduhepa's reply (the latter preserved in the Hittite state archives), provides an insight into his private thoughts and character: "My Sister wrote to me, 'I will send you a daughter,' yet you still hold back from me, unkindly. Why have you not yet given her to me?"[9] Not for the last time in history, a mighty ruler comes across as having a rather thin skin, ever on the alert for slights, real or perceived.

Puduhepa sent back an equally testy reply, reproaching Ramesses for his impatience and avarice — for, probably correctly, she interpreted his real interest as being the dowry, not the princess. To illustrate her point, Puduhepa also referred to a Babylonian princess who had been taken into Ramesses' harem some time earlier but whom, according to rumor, Babylonian envoys had subsequently been prevented from visiting. This is the only known reference to Ramesses' Babylonian wife, but there is no reason to doubt the veracity of Puduhepa's account: as far back as the reign of Amenhotep III, the kings of Babylon had sent their daughters to marry Egyptian pharaohs to cement friendly relations between the two countries.

At this point in the correspondence, Ramesses — or more likely his wise advisers — recognized that there was nothing to be gained by further antagonizing the Hittite queen. So a suitably diplomatic reply was sent to Puduhepa: "I have seen the tablet that my Sister sent me, and I have noted all the matters on which the Great Queen of Hatti, my sister, has so very, very graciously written to me. . . . The Great King, the King of Hatti, my brother, has written to me saying, 'Let the people come, to pour fine oil upon my daughter's head, and may she be brought into the house of the Great King, the King of Egypt!' . . . Excellent, excellent is this decision . . . two great countries will become as one land, forever!"[10] Ramesses duly sent an envoy to Hattusa to anoint the princess's head with oil, formally signifying her betrothal to the pharaoh.

The journey of the Hittite princess from her lofty royal citadel in central Anatolia through the hills and valleys of the Levant, and her arrival at Per-Ramesses, are recounted in detail in a commemorative inscription which Ramesses had carved at Abu Simbel (twice — inside and outside the Great Temple), Amara, Elephantine, and Karnak. In keeping with tradition, official ideology, and Ramesses' self-image, the marriage was presented as an act of submission by the Hittites: "The Great King of Hatti wrote to satisfy His Majesty. . . . 'With my eldest daughter in front of them, let us carry divine offerings to the King of Egypt so that he may give us peace and we may live.' . . . Then he had his eldest daughter brought, the noble tribute before her consisting of gold, silver, bronze, countless slaves, horses without limit, cattle, goats, rams."[11]

The account relates how Ramesses prayed to Seth for good weather to accompany the princess on her journey south, whereupon "the sky was calm and summer days occurred in winter." Like earlier tales of Ramesses' well digging and quarrying prowess, this detail was included to emphasize his declared ability to control the forces of nature. The bridal train "traversed remote mountains and difficult passes" before reaching the Egyptian frontier, where it was met by a detachment of the Egyptian army and various court officials. At last, in the third month of winter (early January), the princess arrived at Per-Ramesses: "Then the daughter of the Great Ruler of Hatti was ushered . . . into the presence of His Majesty, with very great tribute in her train, without limit, all manner of things. Then His Majesty saw her as one fair of face, first among women. . . . Behold, it was a great and mysterious event, a precious marvel, never known or heard of in popular tradition, never recounted in writing, since the time of the forefathers: the daughter of the Great Ruler of Hatti coming, proceeding to Egypt, to the Dual King Usermaatra-setepenra, the son of Ra Ramesses-beloved-of-Amun, given life." The Hittite princess was given an Egyptian name, Maathorneferura ("She who sees Horus, the beauty of Ra"), which referenced her new husband and signaled her primary role as an accoutrement of the divine pharaoh. She was depicted on

Egyptian monuments as a fully fledged Egyptian consort. In her case, however, unlike that of her unfortunate Babylonian predecessor, the match seems to have worked on a personal, as well as a diplomatic level: Ramesses' official account of the marriage ends with the words, "Now she was beautiful in His Majesty's heart and he loved her more than anything."

PATERFAMILIAS

Ramesses' marriage to Hattusili's eldest daughter ushered in a golden age in Egyptian-Hittite relations. The two royal families, now intimately connected, continued the regular correspondence that had begun at the time of the peace treaty. So cordial was the relationship, and so stable the resulting political situation in the Levant, that "if a man or a woman went on business to Syria, they could reach the land of Hatti without fear in their hearts."[12] Indeed, the route between Hattusa and Per-Ramesses was deemed so secure that the Hittite crown prince Hishmi-Sharruma (later King Tudhaliya IV) visited Egypt on at least one occasion. Like his sister before him, he traveled in the winter months – a fact remarked upon by Ramesses in a subsequent letter to Hattusili III – and returned to Hatti in the spring, laden with presents.

The evident success of this visit seems to have paved the way for an official invitation to be sent to the Hittite ruler himself. The surviving correspondence indicates that Hattusili initially gave the invitation a cool reception, prompting Ramesses to suggest as an alternative a summit meeting of the two rulers in Canaan. Hattusili seems to have been won round, only to have to cancel the plans as a result of a painful affliction, termed "burning of the feet" (possibly gout). Whether the two mighty kings ever did meet, "brother seeing brother," is not known, although there are tantalizing fragments of circumstantial evidence to suggest that they did. In any case, by the fifth decade of his reign, Ramesses was firmly established in the courts of the Near East as well as throughout the Nile Valley as the most respected and venerable ruler of the age. His standing in international circles was then further enhanced with the dispatch from Hattusa of a second Hittite princess, another of Hattusili's daughters, to add to the pharaoh's growing harem: "The Great Ruler of Hatti sent the many and abundant spoils of Hatti, the many and abundant spoils of Keshkesh, the many and abundant spoils of Arzawa, the many and abundant spoils of Qode, which were unknown in writing, to the Dual King Usermaatra-setepenra, the son of Ra Ramesses-beloved-of-Amun; and likewise many droves of horses, many herds of cattle, many flocks of goats, and many droves of game, before his other daughter, whom he sent to the Dual King Usermaatra-setepenra, the son of Ra Ramesses-beloved-of-Amun, to Egypt, on what was the second [such] occasion."[13] Unlike her older sister, however, this latest diplomatic bride seems to have found less favor with Ramesses. She was never accorded the title "king's great wife" and her name is nowhere recorded.

She may well have followed the path of earlier minor wives by being sent to the harem palace of Merwer (present-day Gurob). Established centuries earlier in a pleasant location by the shores of Lake Fayum, Merwer was a formidable institution in its own right. The royal women who lived there maintained their own household, managed their own estates, and even ran their own enterprise (the manufacture and weaving of fine linen). It was a prosperous but secluded existence: a gilded cage for the pharaoh's lesser wives. Ramesses founded a temple there, and Maathorneferura, his first Hittite bride, is known to have retired to Merwer, perhaps after the initial blush of romance had faded. A fragment of her laundry list was discovered in the palace ruins, referring to rolls of linen "28 cubits and 4 palms long, and 4 cubits wide."[14] We also know that Maathorneferura bore her husband at least one daughter, and the palace at Merwer would have echoed to the cries of babies and small children, the progeny of the pharaoh's many concubines. His sons by lesser wives and his daughters would have spent their childhoods in the palace by the lake. And children there were in abundance.

One of the novel features of Ramesses' reign is the prominence given to his children on royal monuments and in official inscriptions. In earlier eras, the king's offspring were largely invisible, neither seen nor heard. Probably they were deemed to pose too great a threat to the position of the king himself: it would have been all too easy for would-be rebels to rally round one of the king's sons as a focus of discontent. The harem palace, with its personal rivalries and claustrophobic atmosphere, is known to have been the setting for more than one such plot over the course of ancient Egyptian history. Only the crown prince was deemed safe to elevate in the public consciousness, and even then the institution of co-regency was instituted as a safeguard against an overly ambitious heir and to ensure a smooth succession. For most of pharaonic history, therefore, the number and identities of the king's children remain barely known, reconstructed through fleeting references in minor inscriptions. But Ramesses II's status as father of the nation became inextricably linked with his role as paterfamilias. To vaunt his fertility as well as to establish the dynastic credentials of his family, he not only acknowledged, he positively celebrated his prodigious number of offspring. In his temples and inscriptions, from every part of his reign, his numerous children are depicted, named, and listed: some one hundred in all.

Starting with his daughters, the first, borne by Isetnofret before Ramesses' accession, was Bintanat. Her name is Semitic, meaning "daughter of [the goddess] Anat," underscoring the cosmopolitan character of Ramesside Egypt. As the king's eldest daughter and thus a royal heiress, Bintanat played a prominent role in the affairs of state. She was frequently depicted on monuments, from Per-Ramesses to Nubia. And at or about the time of her mother's death, she took on the duties of the king's great wife. Nor was this purely ceremonial: Bintanat is known to have borne her father-husband at least one child, a daughter, who subsequently married Ramesses' eventual successor to maintain the purity of the nineteenth-dynasty family line. Bintanat herself probably outlived her father, surviving into her brother's reign.

Of Bintanat's fifty-odd sisters and half-sisters, only a few emerge as more than names. (The names themselves are fascinating, ranging from the touching—Sithiryotes, "her father's daughter," and Meretmihapi, "beloved like the inundation"—to the pious: Meretptah, "beloved of Ptah," and Sitamun, "daughter of Amun.") One of the best known is Meritamun, Ramesses' fourth daughter (by Nefertari), who shared Bintanat's official duties after their mothers' deaths and was lauded as "splendid of features, magnificent in the place, beloved of the Lord of the Two Lands, she who stands by her master like Sirius is beside Orion."[15] Two other daughters who served as the king's great wife, Nebettawy and Henuttawy, were included in the official decorative scheme at Abu Simbel. Other royal women similarly celebrated at the site include Ramesses' mother, Tuya; his two principal consorts, Nefertari and Isetnofret; his two oldest daughters, Bintanat and Baketmut; and a later, evidently favored, daughter, Nefertari II, named after her mother.

More prominent in the record are Ramesses' sons, especially

those born early in his adult life to Nefertari and Isetnofret. The equal status of the two wives, at least in the king's eyes, is shown by the fact that their sons ranked in order of birth, irrespective of the mother. Processions of princes are depicted on many of Ramesses' monuments, notably the outer wall of the hypostyle hall at Karnak, the temple of Beit el-Wali, and the Ramesseum, together with further scenes of the royal children at Abu Simbel, Derr, Wadi es-Sebua, Luxor Temple, and the temple of Seti I at Abydos.

Ramesses' first son (born to Nefertari) arrived during the reign of Seti I, when Ramesses was still heir apparent. He was given the name Amunhirwenemef, "Amun is at his right hand," and seems to have played a part—if only ceremonial—in the Nubian skirmish commemorated on the walls of Beit el-Wali. Also shown in the temple's battle reliefs is Ramesses' fourth son, Khaemwaset (born to Isetnofret). Neither boy can have been more than a few years old, so their depiction cannot reflect the realities of battle. When Ramesses acceded to the throne, Amunhirwenemef was officially recognized as "king's eldest son" (heir apparent) and his name was altered slightly to the more martial-sounding Amunhirkhepeshef, "Amun is at his sword arm." Certainly, destiny and duty dictated an army career for the lad. In the temple of Seti I at Abydos he is shown with his father lassoing a bull, a metaphor for subduing the forces of chaos. Real military action was not long in coming: the prince evidently participated in the Battle of Kadesh—by which time he was probably in his early teens—and was rewarded with the title of commander-in-chief. Indeed, every one of Ramesses II's four successive heirs held the title, continuing a tradition that had begun with Horemheb, and proudly proclaiming the military character of the nineteenth dynasty. A fragmentary inscription in Luxor Temple, recording a Moabite campaign of Ramesses II, has the king addressing Amunhirkhepeshef thus: "The king speaks to the crown prince and king's eldest son, Amun-hirkhepeshef: 'Speak with the [chief] of the foreigners — cause that he understand his evil deed.'"[16]

Amunhirkhepeshef remained heir apparent and crown prince for at least the first twenty, perhaps the first twenty-five, years of his father's reign. Under a different, northern form of his name, Sethhirkhepeshef, he is recorded as having played a ceremonial role in the signing of the peace treaty with the Hittites at Per-Ramesses in the twenty-first regnal year.[17] Not long afterward, Amunhirkhepeshef/Sethhirkhepeshef disappears from view. Like many of his compatriots, he probably succumbed to illness, accident, or disease. Dying in one's early thirties was not uncommon in pharaonic Egypt.

Ramesses' second son (born to Isetnofret) was named after his father — another indication, surely, of the esteem in which the king held his "secondary" wife. Like his older half-brother, Prince Ramesses joined the army and participated in the Battle of Kadesh, following which he was promoted to "first general-in-chief." He also held high civilian office, serving as a judge at the trial of a treasury official accused of stealing from the royal stores. After Amunhirkhepeshef's death, Prince Ramesses became heir to the throne and held this status for the next quarter-century until he, too, predeceased his father.

The third son, Prahirwenemef ("Ra is at his right hand," born to Nefertari), followed a similar path to that of his two older siblings. After Kadesh, he held the titles "first soldier of the army" and "first charioteer," but he seems to have died young while still in his twenties. (It is notable that the sons of Isetnofret apparently lived considerably longer than their half-brothers.) Other casualties by this time included Ramesses' ninth and eleventh sons, Sety and Meryra. The former, according to the official account, had participated in the siege of Dapur in Ramesses' tenth regnal year, together with at least four of his brothers: Montuhirkhepeshef (fifth son), Ramesses-Meryamun (seventh son), Amenemwia (eighth son), and Setepenra (tenth son). Amenemwia, under the alternate name Sethemwia, later took part in a military campaign to suppress a minor rebellion in Nubia which broke out while his father was celebrating the peace treaty with the Hittites. This skirmish, which resulted in the capture of seven thousand rebels, also gave an early taste of battle to the pharaoh's thirteenth son, Merenptah; the triumphant aftermath was recorded on the main gate of the fortified Egyptian settlement at Amara West, which was named "Ramesses the Town."

The precise level of involvement of young royal sons in military maneuvers is difficult to ascertain. Given the importance to Ramesses of dynastic succession, it seems unlikely that he would have intentionally put his heirs in harm's way, notwithstanding the overt militaristic tone and character of the dynasty. More likely, perhaps, princes would have watched pitched battles from a safe distance or merely joined in the victory parade once a battle had been safely won. But it suited the official propaganda to have them depicted as active participants in military activity.

Other princes with noteworthy, if rather more peaceable, careers include the sixteenth son, Meryatum, who visited Sinai on a mining expedition during his father's second decade on the throne, accompanied by Ashahebsed, the project manager of the Abu Simbel temples. Although the purpose of the expedition is not known for certain, it is likely to have been to procure supplies of copper and turquoise—both mined in the mountains of Sinai—for the temples' fittings. After proving himself on this commission, Meryatum was appointed "Greatest of Seers," the high priest of Ra at Heliopolis, in which office he continued, loyally, for about two decades. By contrast, Samontu, Ramesses' twenty-third son, served in a more humdrum capacity as administrator of the royal vineyard at Memphis. He is better remembered for his marriage to the daughter of a Syrian ship captain. Perhaps Samontu met her in the port of Memphis, where, as we know from the tomb of Pabes (see above, Chapter 3), ships from across the eastern Mediterranean docked to unload their wares and take on board diverse export goods from Egypt. And then there was Ramesses-Meryamun-Nebweben, the king's forty-sixth son, who had the misfortune to be born a hunchback and lived most of his life in the royal nursery and harem palace at Merwer. There he died, in his thirties, and was buried in the local cemetery in a reused coffin, originally made for his great-grandfather, Ramesses I.

Most of Ramesses II's other sons are little known, recorded in lists but without further detail. Amenhotep (fourteenth son) and Thutmose (twenty-second) were given names harking back to the glory days of the eighteenth dynasty. A clutch of later sons, Samontu (twenty-third), Montuemwaset (twenty-fourth), and Montuen-heqau (twenty-eighth), honored the Theban war god, Montu, emphasizing the nineteenth dynasty's military origins. Other important deities in the wide pantheon of Ramesside religion, such as Horus and Astarte, were referenced in the names of Horhir-wenemef (twelfth) and Astarthirwenemef. And many of the pharaoh's youngest offspring bore names that paid homage to their father, by now a living god in his own right: Ramesses-Meretmirra ("Ramesses beloved like Ra"), Ramesses-Maatptah ("Ramesses the truth of Ptah"), Ramesses-Userpehty ("Ramesses great of strength") and Ramesses-Payotnetjer ("Ramesses the divine father").

For a man so concerned with ensuring the succession, it is perhaps odd that Ramesses II never appointed a formal co-regent;

perhaps he began to believe in his own godlike status. He did, however, ensure that it was always clear who held the position of crown prince: first Amunhirkhepeshef, then his son Ramesses, then the fourth son, Khaemwaset, and finally the thirteenth son, Merenptah. Indeed, it would be these last two — both the children of Isetnofret, not Nefertari — who would play the most prominent roles in their father's reign, the latter eventually succeeding to the throne, having outlived his twelve older brothers.

PAST, PRESENT, AND FUTURE

While his extensive progeny secured the future, Ramesses II had a conflicted attitude toward the past. On one hand, he was eager to demonstrate the legitimacy of his dynasty by drawing on historical precedent, whether in the formulation of his throne name, the construction of Luxor Temple, or the naming of his sons. It is no coincidence that one of his first acts on becoming king was to order the erection of two stelae at Giza (one in Khafra's valley temple, already over a thousand years old) and a shrine between the paws of the Great Sphinx; together, these monuments marked Ramesses' accession and confirmed his right to rule in continuation of a tradition first established in the eighteenth dynasty. On the other hand, the plebeian, provincial origins of his family, and its unorthodox path to power — as the ultimate beneficiary of a series of dynastic crises following in the wake of Akhenaten's heretical reign and the untimely death of his son Tutankhamun — were not facts to be trumpeted, but rather glossed over by pomp and propaganda.

What was true of the past was also true of the present. In some senses, the nineteenth dynasty presented itself as a breath of fresh air: a new, vigorous, military family to sweep away memories of the effete and ineffectual rulers of the late eighteenth dynasty. Yet at the same time, the aspects of pharaonic art and ideology that Ramesses and his artisans most keenly adopted and promoted, such as a more realistic depiction of the human figure, or the elevation of the royal family into a focus of popular worship, were innovations of the very king (Akhenaten) whose monuments Ramesses finally razed into oblivion.

This Janus-like aspect of Ramesses' reign, with one eye on its inheritance and another on its legacy, is exemplified in the life and career of his fourth son, Khaemwaset.[18] Unlike the other royal princes, Khaemwaset has survived the vicissitudes of history to emerge as a powerful personality in his own right, a son of Ramesses who sheds light on, rather than being overshadowed by, his father. Khaemwaset ("Risen in Thebes') was born to Isetnofret during the reign of Seti I, when Ramesses was still co-regent. As a boy of five or six, Khaemwaset was present for the Nubian campaign that was immortalized on the walls of the temple at Beit el-Wali. Eight or nine years later, he took part, perhaps more actively, in the siege of Dapur, as depicted on the walls of the Ramesseum. But an army life does not seem to have been Khaemwaset's calling. The indications are that he was a man of letters, not a man of war. As a youth he entered the priesthood, rising swiftly to the rank of sem-priest (an ancient religious role with strong connections to the ideology of divine kingship) and deputy to the high priest of Ptah, Huy. This last office took Khaemwaset to Memphis.

Although the city must have changed much in the eighteen centuries since its foundation, the monuments of past kings—especially those of the Pyramid Age—still loomed large on the horizon. From south to north, all along the edge of the western escarpment, the great stone edifices erected by the rulers of the third, fourth, fifth, and sixth dynasties dominated the landscape. By the reign of Ramesses II, the Memphite necropolis had become something of a tourist attraction. Graffiti written by ancient visitors include an inscription left by a scribe named Nashuyu when he came "to the district of the pyramid of Teti . . . and the pyramid of Djoser" and another, on the latter monument itself, which recounts how "the scribe of the Treasury Hednakht, son of Tjuneroy and Tawosret, came to take a stroll and relax in the west of Memphis, along with his brother Panakht, scribe of the vizier."[19]

From his base in the temple of Ptah at Memphis, Khaemwaset took a strong personal interest in the monuments of the past that he saw all around him. Indeed, he did not merely visit the ancient pyramids as a casual tourist; he seems to have observed them as a student of history, determined to restore those he found in a poor state. When he succeeded Huy to the position of high priest of Ptah (designated by the ancient title "Greatest of Craftsmen"), he was able to command the resources needed to carry out his restoration plans. No fewer than six major royal complexes — ranging in age from the third-dynasty step pyramid of Djoser to the fifth-dynasty pyramid of Unas — bear witness to Khaemwaset's conservation activities. From south Saqqara (the sarcophagus-shaped tomb of the fourth-dynasty king Shepseskaf) all the way to Abusir (the sun temple of the fifth-dynasty king Niuserra), monuments of the Pyramid Age were systematically repaired and given new inscriptions describing the work. On the pyramid of Unas, for example, giant hieroglyphs were carved to tell posterity: "His Majesty commanded the Greatest of Craftsmen, sem-priest and king's son Khaemwaset to restore the name of the Dual King Unas, for lo, his name was not found upon his great pyramid. So the sem-priest and king's son Khaemwaset restored the monuments of the divine kings and monarchs."[20] For the name of a monument's creator not to be found prominently displayed on its facade must have been anathema to a son of Ramesses II.

Nor were Khaemwaset's attentions confined to large, public monuments. His genuine antiquarian interest was also sparked by much smaller vestiges of the past. When investigating the ruined fourth-dynasty tombs of high officials that surrounded the pyramids at Giza, he came across a statue of Kawab, a son of King Khufu, builder of the Great Pyramid. This image of a royal prince from more than a thousand years earlier seems to have struck a particular chord with Khaemwaset. He added his own inscription to the piece, describing the circumstances of its discovery and restoration: "It was the Greatest of Craftsmen, sem-priest and king's son who restored this statue of the king's son Kawab."[21] He then reinstated the statue in a chapel in the Memphite necropolis. The inscriptions show an accurate understanding of the place in history of Kawab, Khufu, and the next king of the fourth dynasty, Khafra. By means of such close attention to the remains of antiquity in his backyard, Khaemwaset seems to have developed his interest into scholarship. On some of his monuments, he tried to copy the style of the Pyramid Age reliefs; on others he carved learned, even archaic texts reflecting a detailed knowledge of ancient writings. For these reasons, Khaemwaset has been called, with some justification, the first Egyptologist.

His fascination with the monuments of yore achieved its ultimate expression in an enigmatic construction of his own design, which he had erected on a hilltop site between North Saqqara and Abusir.[22] The site had a splendid view of the entire necropolis: on a clear day all the pyramids from Dahshur in the south to Giza in the north were visible from the rocky eminence. The building, now systematically plundered and destroyed, seems originally to have comprised three main elements, arranged east to west. An impressive portico with two rows of stone columns with lotus-bud capitals faced east, toward the rising sun. In its design, it recalled the temple-like tomb chapels of the late eighteenth dynasty, notably the Memphite tomb of Horemheb. The portico led to a rectangular corridor, which connected with the rearmost part of the building, a small cult chamber some six feet square. The decoration of this room included a beautiful limestone "false door" (offering niche), carved in exemplary workmanship with an image of the ancient Memphite god of the underworld, Sokar, and the names and titles of Khaemwaset. Fragments of a second false door, carved from granite, likewise bore the imprint of "the Greatest of Craftsmen, sem-priest and king's son, Khaemwaset." Elsewhere in the chamber were scenes of the sun god Ra-Horakhty, and an amulet depicting the god of sunlight, Shu, was found nearby. Combining reverence to the chthonic deity of the necropolis with praises to the rising sun and its daily promise of resurrection, Khaemwaset's hilltop sanctuary can be interpreted as the architectural expression of his own beliefs — beliefs which were shaped by the remains of Egypt's remote antiquity that he studied so assiduously.

This fascination with the past, and especially with the rulers of old, is manifested in another characteristic feature of Ramesses II's reign: the preponderance of king lists. A major element of the decoration of Seti I's temple at Abydos, which Ramesses completed, was the hall of ancestors, listing every recognized king of Egypt all the way back to Menes, the legendary founder of the first dynasty. Ramesses evidently liked the feature so much that he had a copy carved in his own adjacent temple at Abydos. It is likely that other major temples, too, had similar inscriptions. The existence of a king list in the temple of Ptah at Memphis seems to be suggested by the inclusion of an abbreviated version in a nearby private tomb, that of Tjuneroy. Tjuneroy's roles as "overseer of works on all the

monuments of the king" and "chief controller of all the monuments of the king" meant that he may well have supervised Khaemwaset's restoration projects, and he would certainly have had an
intimate knowledge of the ancient pyramids and tombs of the
Memphite necropolis. Tjuneroy also held the post of lector-priest,
which would have given him access to the religious texts kept in
the temple scriptorium, and sem-priest of the king, which would
have afforded him a detailed understanding of royal ritual and
precedent. Bringing all this knowledge and experience together,
Tjuneroy decorated his tomb chapel at Saqqara with a selective list
of fifty-eight kings, beginning (strangely) with Merpabia Anedjib,
the sixth king of the first dynasty, and ending with the reigning
monarch, Ramesses II. The tainted rulers from Akhenaten to Ay
were excluded, as was Hatshepsut, the female pharaoh of the earlier eighteenth dynasty, and the hated Hyksos. The list also omit-
ted the ephemeral kings of the ninth/tenth, and thirteenth to sev-
enteenth dynasties. The kings of the eleventh and twelfth dynasties
were placed in reverse order, betraying a certain confusion over
their proper sequence. By contrast, the list of fourth-dynasty kings,
nine monarchs in total, is the most extensive known from ancient
Egypt; it suggests that Tjuneroy, like Khaemwaset, enjoyed an en-
cyclopedic knowledge of the builders of the Pyramid Age, based on
firsthand experience. Also listed comprehensively are the little-
known kings of the early and mid-second dynasty, whose monuments, now lost, probably stood at Saqqara and would have been
known to Tjuneroy. From such details, it is clear that his king list
is no mere copy or amateur imitation; rather, it is an original
chronology, based on primary sources that were not only still available but also carefully curated and studied.

The ultimate expression of this antiquarian interest is to be
found in the most complete king list to have survived from ancient

Egypt, the papyrus known today as the Turin Canon (after the Museo Egizio in Turin, where it is housed). Compiled, like its counterparts at Abydos and Saqqara in the reign of Ramesses II, it seems to represent a genuine attempt at historiography. The medium on which it is written — friable papyrus rather than permanent stone — allowed the scribe to aim for historical accuracy, rather than sanitized propaganda. Unique among the surviving king lists, the Turin Canon records all the minor, contested, and dubious monarchs of Egypt alongside the officially sanctioned heroes of the past. Hence, while Tjuneroy's list runs to 58 kings, and the Abydos list to 76, the Turin Canon has no fewer than 223 royal names. Some of these are mythical — gods, demi-gods, and spirits that were believed to have reigned before the first human monarch — but the remainder, beginning with Menes and ending before the expulsion of the Hyksos, are known, historical figures. The information, which includes reign lengths and in some cases the lifespans of monarchs, seems to have been drawn from a variety of historical sources, suggesting a work of true scholarly research. This is also indicated by the headings and summations, which divide the list into groupings of kings, broadly equating to the periods and dynasties employed by modern historians (which date back to a history of Egypt compiled by a priest named Manetho in the third century B.C.). Written on the back of a tax register, the Turin Canon remains something of an enigma. Whether it was compiled for official purposes or by a scribe with access to historical records is uncertain. Whatever its purpose, it reinforces the impression that the court of Ramesses II was an environment in which an interest in the past was officially sanctioned — and actively encouraged.

As deputy high priest, then high priest of Ptah, Khaemwaset would have been familiar with one particularly ancient custom, the cult of the Apis bull. According to a belief which stretched back to the beginning of Egyptian history, a bull with special markings was worshipped as the avatar of the god Ptah, kept in a special compound at Memphis, and visited by pilgrims from far and wide. Each bull at its death would be mummified and buried with full honors in a special tomb in the Saqqara necropolis.[23] A new Apis would then be identified by the priests of Ptah, and the cycle would begin again. As deputy high priest, Khaemwaset would have witnessed the burial of an Apis bull in the sixteenth year of Ramesses' reign. Succeeding to the position of Greatest of Craftsmen, Khaemwaset duly found himself presiding over the next Apis burial fourteen years later. Until this time, each successive bull had been buried in a separate chamber. But Khaemwaset decided to set a new precedent by interring the latest deceased Apis alongside its immediate predecessor in the same tomb. (These are the only Apis burials to have been discovered intact, still lying in their immense black wooden coffins, adorned with gold jewelry bearing the names of Ramesses II and Khaemwaset.) Evolving the concept further, the prince then founded new underground galleries, a veritable catacomb, where successive bulls could be interred side by side. The first Apis was buried in the new gallery in Ramesses' fifty-fifth regnal year, and Khaemwaset intended it to serve for the rest of time. (This was also, in all likelihood, earmarked as his own burial place.) In all practical senses, he achieved his ambition, for the Serapeum, as it came to be called, remained in use for a thousand years. A lengthy inscription carved at the entrance explained Khaemwaset's motivation for founding the hypogeum (underground burial chamber) and its accompanying temple:

> I am a valiant heir, a vigilant champion, excelling in wisdom according to Thoth. . . . Never has the like happened, the recording in writing in the great festival court before this temple. . . . I have established for him

the divine offerings: daily offerings every day, festivals of heaven whose days come around on their appointed dates, and calendar festivals throughout the year. . . . I have [built] for him a great stone shrine before his temple, to rest in it during the day when preparing for burial. I have made for him a great altar before his great shrine, of fine Tura limestone. . . . It will indeed seem to you a benefaction when you look upon what the ancestors have done, poor and ignorant works. . . . Remember my name. . . . I am the sem-priest and king's son.[24]

A fascination with antiquity, an obsession with legitimacy, but also a determination to establish new traditions: the career and monuments of Khaemwaset offer an illuminating perspective on his father's reign, a time of tradition and innovation.

TOGETHER FOREVER

By the time Khaemwaset inaugurated the Serapeum, he had already served as high priest of Ptah for perhaps a quarter of a century and was the third crown prince of his father's reign. Ramesses II's sheer longevity not only prevented a series of heirs from succeeding to the throne, it must also have enhanced the monarch's godlike status in the eyes of his subjects. Since the dawn of Egyptian history, the thirtieth year of a reign, an uncommon occurrence at the best of times, had been marked by a jubilee, called a *sed*-festival. Not many rulers had lived long enough to hold such a celebration. Only one king, Amenhotep III, had presided over three jubilees. (Subsequent jubilees were held every three years.) But in time Ramesses II would celebrate no fewer than fourteen.

His first sed-festival, held according to ancient custom in his thirtieth year on the throne, was proclaimed, not as tradition dic-

tated from the royal citadel at Memphis, but in the columned jubilee hall at Per-Ramesses. It must have seemed appropriate for
such a landmark event to be launched at the king's dynastic seat.
However, Ramesses' was a geographically extensive realm, and
such an important occasion demanded formal announcements at
every major site. The man entrusted with the task was Khaemwaset, and he seems to have fulfilled his duties admirably. He
traveled the length of the Nile Valley, issuing proclamations from
Memphis to Elephantine. The gods seemed to show their approval
when the first sed-festival was accompanied by a particularly boun-
teous inundation; Khaemwaset celebrated the phenomenon with
commemorative stelae erected at the First Nile Cataract and at
Gebel el-Silsila, locations closely connected with the annual Nile
flood. At the latter site, Khaemwaset also paid homage to his
mother, depicting Ramesses and Isetnofret with their four most
prominent children: Bintanat, Ramesses, Khaemwaset himself,
and Merenptah.

The same pattern of proclamations was followed for the king's
next four jubilees, celebrated in his thirty-fourth, thirty-seventh,
fortieth, and forty-third regnal years, with Khaemwaset acting as
master of ceremonies; he took the opportunity to place statues of
his own in the principal temples of the land, including Abydos and
Karnak. Later jubilees seem to have attracted less attention, their
proclamation delegated to a vizier – perhaps the court and country
alike grew a little tired of the triennial jamborees – and in any case
Khaemwaset himself was growing older and less vigorous. During
his time as high priest of Ptah, he had fathered his own family:
his eldest son was named Ramesses, a daughter was Isetnofret; a
younger son, Hori, followed in his father's footsteps, becoming
Greatest of Craftsmen in turn. Around the fifty-fifth year of Ramesses' reign, when Khaemwaset had been crown prince for five

years, and just after he had inaugurated his lasting monument, the Serapeum, he died. The site of his tomb is not known for certain but is likely to have been in his beloved Memphite necropolis, perhaps even within the Serapeum itself, alongside the sacred Apis bulls.

The new crown prince, who would effectively rule Egypt for the final decade of his father's reign, was Ramesses' thirteenth son and Khaemwaset's younger full brother, Merenptah. He had never expected to become heir apparent. Earlier in the reign, he had been described, somewhat dismissively, as "younger brother" to Bintanat, Prince Ramesses, and Khaemwaset. He seems to have married his niece, Khaemwaset's daughter Isetnofret (and, in turn, their son would marry his own aunt), perhaps suggesting an especially close bond between the two brothers. Like most royal princes, Merenptah was given military titles, but he only came to prominence on becoming first in line to the throne. During his decade or so as king in waiting, as his aging father reigned on and on, his thoughts must have turned to the day when Ramesses would eventually join his ancestors in the necropolis. As heir, it would fall to Merenptah to preside at Ramesses' burial. Everything had to be ready.

Fortunately, Ramesses had left nothing to chance in preparing for the afterlife. He had, after all, had plenty of time to plan appropriate tombs for himself and his extensive family — sepulchers that drew on centuries of royal tradition while also displaying a characteristic streak of Ramesside innovation.[25] Tradition dictated that Thebes was the proper place for royal burials, yet under the nineteenth dynasty the town was becoming increasingly remote, not to say peripheral, for rulers who spent most of their time in the north (at Memphis or Per-Ramesses) and who had no ancestral connections with the south of the country. Nonetheless, just as Ramesses had commissioned a memorial temple at western Thebes (the Ramesseum), so he decided to follow precedent and excavate the royal tombs in its remote wadis. What was new was his definition of *royal*.

Since the beginning of the eighteenth dynasty, pharaohs had been interred in the Valley of the Kings, but far less attention had been given to their wives. Indeed, most queenly burials of the period remain unidentified. Ramesses, with his evident fondness for women and his close relationships with successive great wives, took a much more planned and systematic approach to the interment of female members of his family. In the early eighteenth dynasty, a distinct necropolis in the hills of western Thebes, known as *ta set neferu,* "the place of beauties," had been chosen for minor members of the royal family. At the beginning of the nineteenth dynasty, Ramesses I had built a tomb there for his wife, Satra. His grandson Ramesses II now transformed the burial ground (known today as the Valley of the Queens) into an exclusive resting place for royal consorts.

Three reasons may have lain behind his choice. First, the valley was particularly associated with Hathor, divine mother and goddess of the western mountain; a shrine to Hathor stood at the entrance to the valley, while a dramatic cleft in the rocks at its westernmost end resembles a vulva. Second, after a rainstorm, water pours out of the cleft, giving the area a surreal atmosphere that may have heightened its divine associations. Third, and most prosaically, the valley is located close to the village of the necropolis workers, known to the ancient Egyptians as "the Place of Truth" (modern Deir el-Medina). Given that in Ramesses' reign the workers were employed simultaneously in excavating and decorating tombs for the king and several members of his family, practical considerations such as ease of access may have been as important as mystical connotations.

While the earliest tombs in the valley had been cut into the southern side, Ramesses ordered the burials for his female relatives to be excavated in the northern slope. The first such monument, and the finest, was created for the king's first and favorite wife, Nefertari. It remains the best-preserved example of a consort's tomb from ancient Egypt. In its layout it resembles a condensed version of a king's burial, without the long corridors between chambers. The ceiling is painted dark blue with golden stars to resemble the night sky, and the walls depict Nefertari's progress from death to rebirth in the realm of Osiris. The decoration follows the general scheme of a king's tomb, though it does not encroach on subjects considered the monarch's prerogative. Hence the afterlife book known as *Amduat* (what is in the underworld) does not appear; in its place are extracts from the *Book of Gates* and the *Book of Going Forth by Day* (also known as the *Book of the Dead*), the latter more commonly associated with private tombs of the Ramesside period. Nefertari's sepulcher thus occupies a space somewhere between a royal and a nonroyal tomb, with strong regal overtones. Subsequent tombs in the Valley of the Queens were created for Ramesses' mother, Tuya; his daughter-wives Bintanat, Meritamun, Nebettawy, and Henuttawy; and two other daughters, Henutmira and an unnamed princess.[26] The most intensive period of activity seems to have been between the death of Nefertari and Ramesses' fortieth regnal year; during this time, a temporary village was built in the middle of the valley to house the workers during the week and obviate the need for them to travel every day from their main settlement at the Place of Truth. This greatly speeded up the pace of work. Later in the reign, however, the number of workmen was sharply reduced and the temporary village disbanded. The tomb of Henutmira was probably the last to be dug in the place of beauties under Ramesses II.

One tomb is notable by its absence from the Valley of the Queens: the burial of Nefertari's great rival, Isetnofret. An ancient ostracon (inscribed fragment of pottery or stone) from Thebes refers to the "tomb of Isetnofret" and suggests a location in the Valley of the Kings; however, the burial in question may have been that of Merenptah's wife, Isetnofret (II), not his mother. The final resting place of Ramesses' second queen has never been found.

Thanks to the remarkable preservation of the Place of Truth, nestled out of sight in its own remote wadi, much is known about the lives and identities of the workers who excavated and decorated the royal tombs of the period. Letters, jottings, and graffiti found in the ruins of the village bring to life the architects, masons, sculptors, and painters who dedicated their careers to preparing everlasting sepulchers for their sovereign and members of his family. During the first third of Ramesses' reign, the man in overall charge of projects in both the Valley of the Queens and Valley of the Kings was the southern vizier, Paser. He had been appointed by Seti I, came from a line of Theban notables (his father had been high priest of Amun), and was made directly responsible for royal works in western Thebes on Ramesses' accession. The surviving correspondence suggests that Paser had a good relationship with the "scribe of the tomb" (the chief administrator of the necropolis workers), and ensured that the workmen received their pay and rations on time. A letter written by the mayor of western Thebes to the site foreman notes, "The vizier Paser has sent to me saying, 'Let the dues be brought for the workmen on the royal tomb, namely vegetables, fish, firewood, jars of beer, food, and milk. Do not let a scrap of it remain outstanding. . . . Do not let me find that you have held back as balance anything that is due. Be careful over this!'"[27]

Artifacts and inscriptions found inside the workmen's village even enable particular dwellings to be assigned to specific individuals. In the older part of the settlement, for example, just inside the main gateway, a house set back a little from the main street and more spacious than most—with two sitting rooms, three bedrooms, and two ancillary rooms—belonged to the chief workman, Qaha (one of the addressees of the letter quoted above), his wife, Tuy, and their eight children. Three doors down on the other side of the street lived the draftsman Maainakhtef, and farther along still a security guard named Khawy. The sculptor Neferrenpet occupied a slightly larger house, with a broad front parlor and two bedroom suites. In the newer, rear extension to the village, the inhabitants included another draftsman, Prahotep, and a number of ordinary workmen.

The workforce employed at any particular time on the royal tomb was organized into two teams, one for the right-hand and one for the left-hand side of the monument. Each team consisted of about thirty men and was led by a foreman assisted by a deputy. The whole "gang," as it was termed, was watched over by two scribes of the tomb, a small squad of police officers, and one or more security guards, and assisted by a small army of water carriers, smiths, and porters, plus a doctor and an expert in scorpion stings (a common hazard for those working among the rocks of the Theban hills).

In a normal reign, the workers would have devoted themselves entirely to work on the royal tomb itself—the biggest and most important project for any king. But Ramesses' tenure on the throne was not normal. During his long years as pharaoh, work proceeded simultaneously on his own tomb, on those of his wives and daughters in the Valley of the Queens, and – last but not least – on a monumental project that dwarfed anything previously attempted in the vicinity. In keeping with Ramesses' emphasis on dynastic succession, and the unprecedented profile afforded his offspring on official monuments, he decided to commission an entirely novel type of tomb in the Valley of the Kings: a burial for his many sons.[28] Commenced in the second decade of his reign, it marked a major innovation in funerary architecture and may have inspired Khaemwaset's subsequent design for the Serapeum at Saqqara.[29] The tomb, known today as KV5, is probably the largest ever made, or discovered, in Egypt. To date – and excavations are still ongoing – over one hundred separate chambers have been located, and there may be as many as fifty more. The tomb is not only bigger than any other in the Nile Valley, it is also unique in plan. A huge entrance hall, its sixteen supporting pillars cut out of the living rock, leads to a corridor one hundred feet long, at the end of which are two transverse corridors, each extending for more than sixty feet. At the junction of the three corridors, a life-size statue of Osiris looms out of the bedrock to greet the visitor. Each of the corridors is lined with rooms or suites of rooms, comprising some forty-eight chambers in total. The walls of the corridors and chambers are decorated in sunk relief, or painted plaster, with scenes of the king presenting his sons to the gods of Egypt – including Sokar (ancient underworld deity of the Memphite necropolis) and Hathor (goddess of the hills of western Thebes). Ramesses, it seems, was covering all bases.

At least twenty-five sons have so far been identified in the images and texts of KV5. The tomb is known for certain to have served as the burial place of Amunhirkhepeshef, Prince Ramesses, Meryamun, and Sety. The burial chambers of other princes may still lie undiscovered, deep inside the mountain, for two additional corridors lead from the front of the pillared hall, plunging downward at a steep angle, each lined with side chambers. No other royal family mausoleum has ever been found in Egypt, and it seems that the tomb of Ramesses' sons gained immediate renown. Such fame was not, however, entirely welcome. A papyrus from several generations later detailing civil unrest across western Thebes describes a robbery which targeted both the tomb of Ramesses II and that of his sons: "Now Userhat and Patwera have stripped stones from above the tomb of the late King Usermaatra-setepenra, the great god. . . . And Kenena son of Ruta did it in the same manner above the tomb of the royal children of the late King Usermaatra-setepenra, the great god."[30]

What this ancient description alludes to, and what twenty-first-century 3-D photogrammetry of the Valley of the Kings has confirmed, is the close connection between the pharaoh's own tomb and the burial of his sons. Although their entrances are located on opposite sides of the main wadi, the passages at the rear of KV5 turn back on the tomb's main axis to descend toward Ramesses' tomb. This means that the deepest portions of KV5, which are likely to contain the burial chambers of the king's principal sons, lie directly adjacent to the pharaoh's final resting place. Ramesses' elevation of the royal family and his self-presentation as the sire of a great dynasty were no passing fads: through systematic development of the Valley of the Queens and spectacular innovation in the Valley of the Kings, he ensured that he would be surrounded by his wives, daughters, and especially sons for all eternity.

CHAPTER FIVE

From Here to Eternity

To judge from the decoration of private tombs, expectations of life beyond the grave seem to have undergone
something of a change with the advent of the nineteenth dynasty.
Whereas the tomb chapels of the eighteenth dynasty are full of
scenes of daily life – agriculture, craft production, and so on – those
of the Ramesside period focus almost exclusively on scenes of a
religious nature. The funerary banquet, for centuries a staple motif,
disappears entirely, to be replaced by more static scenes of the deceased and his wife (nearly all tombs were for men) seated before
offering tables. By contrast, the funerary procession to the tomb
entrance, a rarity in eighteenth-dynasty decorative schemes, becomes commonplace. Deities, too, loom large in the decoration
of Ramesside private tombs. Osiris, god of the dead and lord of
the underworld, is the most frequently depicted, but Ra-Horakhty,
god of the rising sun and bringer of resurrection, is also regularly
encountered. Scenes previously the preserve of the royal tomb also
make their first appearance in private burials of the nineteenth dynasty: the judgment of the dead, other vignettes from the *Book of*

Going Forth by Day, and the spirits of the deceased being attended by a tree goddess. The choice of gods depicted on the walls of a private tomb often seems to reflect the particular religious preference of the owner, suggesting an era which placed as much emphasis on personal piety as on the major state cults. In general, the decoration of Ramesside private tombs is closely linked to specific religious texts and rituals. It indicates that a genuine concern with individual salvation had replaced the eighteenth-dynasty self-confidence in an assured resurrection.

The catalyst for this subtle but important shift in funerary beliefs may have been the shock and aftereffects of Akhenaten's religious revolution, which had denied everyone (except the king and his family) the promise of an afterlife. In overthrowing the old orthodoxy with its comfortable certainties, Akhenaten's religion forced people to rethink their attitudes toward life after death and their personal relationship with the divine.

Customs and practices surrounding the king's burial and expected resurrection were slower to change. Ramesses himself started making preparations for the afterlife almost as soon as he ascended the throne. In his first few months as king, his agents must have begun scouting the Valley of the Kings for a suitable location for the royal tomb. Once this had been identified, at a spot some distance from the burials of Ramesses I and Seti I, closer to the main valley entrance, a silver chisel was used to make the first ritual cut in the rock on the thirteenth day of the second month of winter in the king's second regnal year.[1] So unfamiliar were the necropolis workers with the new royal titulary that they made a mistake in the carving of Ramesses' names next to the entrance, reversing the first two signs of his throne name. (The error was later corrected by plastering over the wall and re-carving it.) But the decoration of the lintel left no doubt about the identity of the owner: it showed the solar disk (standing for Ramesses himself, whom his contemporaries called "the great sun of Egypt") flanked by the goddesses Isis and Nephthys, traditional guardians of the dead.

In its layout, the tomb of Ramesses II (known today as KV7) illustrates the mix of tradition and innovation that characterizes other aspects of his reign.[2] From Akhenaten on, royal tombs were laid out on a single, straight axis, from entrance to burial chamber. Ramesses, however, reverted to the earlier eighteenth-dynasty bent-axis plan. A new departure was the siting of the sunken portion of the burial chamber—which, below a limestone trapdoor, held the materials left over from the mummification—in the center of the room, rather than toward the rear, an arrangement that was followed in subsequent royal tombs. The decoration, too, displayed a blend of old and new features. The basic scheme followed closely that of Seti I's tomb, with a blend of Osirian (afterlife) and solar (rebirth) imagery. The first three descending corridors featured vignettes from a theological work known as the *Litany of Ra*, praising the sun god in all his forms; deeper into the tomb, the walls of the fourth and fifth corridors and their adjacent chambers were covered with extracts from the *Amduat* and the *Book of Gates*, representing the journey of the deceased into the underworld; the "chariot hall" that concludes this first section of the tomb was decorated with scenes and texts related to the twelfth hour of the sun's journey into the underworld. In the second section of the tomb, approaching the burial chamber, the decoration focused on the Opening of the Mouth ritual, by which the mummy of the deceased was magically restored to a living, breathing being. In the antechamber and the burial chamber itself—a magnificent, eight-pillared hall, known to the ancient Egyptians as the House of Gold—the walls displayed more extracts from the *Amduat* and the *Book of Gates*, together with scenes from the *Book of the Heavenly*

Cow (first included in a royal tomb in the reign of Tutankhamun) and several chapters from the *Book of Going Forth by Day*. Inclusion of the last in a royal tomb was unprecedented, and it may suggest that some of the religious concerns felt by Ramesses' subjects were shared by the king himself. Rather touchingly, the tomb also makes space for Nefertari's name in a small recess between the third and fourth corridors.

Archaeological evidence suggests that the tomb as a whole took about a decade to complete. The end result was not as long or as deep as the tomb of Seti I—in this respect, at least, Ramesses did not try to outdo his father—but it still covered an area of 8,800 square feet, with one of the largest burial chambers (at 1,950 square feet) of any Theban royal tomb. Positioned in the center of the chamber was the king's sarcophagus, carved, like that of his father, from a single block of translucent calcite, mummiform in shape, with the recumbent figure of the king in high relief on the lid, and decorated inside and out with incised scenes and texts from the *Book of Gates*, filled with colored pigment. Accompanying the sarcophagus was a canopic chest, likewise carved from a single block of calcite. This was originally placed in a square pit cut into the floor of the burial chamber. Opening off the House of Gold were four more chambers to house the king's funerary equipment, which he would have amassed throughout his reign. Given his nearly seven decades on the throne, and the extent of Egypt's diplomatic and trading links at the time, Ramesses' grave goods must have been unimaginably rich and dazzling. (The treasure of Tutankhamun, by contrast, had been hurriedly gathered together for a relatively weak and ephemeral monarch.) Only fragments survive to hint at their original splendor: servant statuettes (*shabtis*) of wood, bronze, and marble are known from early collections of antiquities, amassed in the nineteenth century, or have been recovered from recent excavations in KV7.

In 1213 B.C., after a reign of sixty-six years and two months, aged about ninety, Ramesses, the living god, passed away. Marine sand found within his mummy wrappings indicates that he died and was embalmed in the north of Egypt, near the coast, most likely at his residence of Per-Ramesses. Seventy days after his death, which probably occurred in August, his thirteenth son, fourth crown prince, and now heir, Merenptah, officiated at the royal interment in the Valley of the Kings. Wearing the leopard-skin sash of a sem-priest, the new king would have performed the Opening of the Mouth ceremony on the mummified body of his father at the tomb entrance. Then the priests and attendants would have hauled the royal coffin on its custom-made sledge down into the tomb, along the corridors, through the chariot hall, and into the House of Gold; installed it in the gleaming sarcophagus; performed the final rites; and left Ramesses in the darkness of the tomb, there to reside for all eternity.

Although the wooden door to the tomb was bolted and sealed, little or no attempt seems to have been made to hide its location from prying eyes. Indeed, the shallow entrance and decorated lintel suggest that unlike earlier royal tombs, that of Ramesses II was never designed to be hidden away; rather it was to remain on show, perhaps even to serve as a place of pilgrimage to perpetuate the name and renown of the mighty pharaoh. Certainly, the whereabouts and identity of the tomb were well known sixty years later, when robbers attempted to enter it by removing stone blocks from above the entrance. Systematic looting of most of the tombs in the Valley of the Kings followed in the breakdown of law and order at the end of the twentieth dynasty, and the mummy of Ramesses II was temporarily removed to another nearby tomb before being transferred to a secret cache in the hills behind the valley.

The tomb itself, once one of the most magnificent spectacles in ancient Egypt, but now stripped of its fabulous contents, has fared no better. Its prominent situation was exacerbated by its environmental vulnerability. The pharaoh's architects had blundered in their choice of location: the rock in this part of the valley turned out to be friable and of inferior quality, with seams of shale underlying the limestone, while the tomb's position near the entrance of the valley was susceptible to flooding. Heavy rains have never been common over western Thebes, but when they do come, they wash tons of loose material down the hillsides. Over the centuries, much of that debris found its way into KV7, where it set hard, like concrete. Any wall paintings that survived the floods were damaged when robbers tried to remove the rock-hard fill. Following the end of the dynastic age, the tomb seems to have remained at least partially open, attracting its first tourists during the Ptolemaic and Roman periods. Graffiti carved into the walls of the first corridor include the names of visitors like Herakleos, Echeboulos of Rhodes, Deilos, and Selaminion of Cyprus.

While the final resting place of Ramesses II was successively robbed, desecrated, and abandoned, the memory and reputation of its owner continued to grow. Following a series of short and contested reigns — the result of Ramesses' own longevity and the large number of his descendants — a new, military dynasty, the twentieth, took power in Egypt twenty-three years after his death. Once again in pharaonic history, an army general, one Sethnakht, rescued the country from impending chaos and established his own family in power. Like the nineteenth dynasty before it, the twentieth looked back to the past to secure its legitimacy. Where Ramesses I and Seti I had sought to emulate and recapture the glories of the eighteenth dynasty, Sethnakht and his successors modeled their kingship on that of Ramesses II. For with towering monuments still prominent the length and breadth of Egypt, Ramesses was the pharaoh everyone wanted to copy. Indeed, Sethnakht named his son and heir in honor of his illustrious forebear. When Ramesses III succeeded as king, he sought to restore the luster of his predecessor's long reign by a thoroughgoing program of imitation. Where Ramesses II had chosen the throne name Usermaatra-setepenra and the epithet meryamun ("beloved of Amun"), Ramesses III combined the best of both in his own throne name, Usermaatra-meryamun. Where Ramesses II had built a magnificent memorial temple in western Thebes, the Ramesseum, Ramesses III did likewise, even reusing blocks from the earlier monument to give his own an immediate aura of legitimacy and power. Ramesses III even named his own children after those of his hero: among his sons were princes called Amunhirkhepeshef, Prahirwenemef, and Khaemwaset; a daughter was called Bintanat.[3] After Ramesses III, every succeeding pharaoh of the twentieth dynasty was likewise named Ramesses (IV–XI), and four of them adopted a throne name starting with Usermaatra; none of them, however, reigned for more than seven years, against Ramesses II's seven decades. A royal name alone was no guarantee of longevity, nor of eminence. Ramesses IV so desperately wanted to be the new Ramesses II that he inscribed a prayer to Osiris in the temple at Abydos – site of the earlier pharaoh's most important dynastic inscriptions – urging the god to grant him a great age and a long reign.[4] But to no avail. He enjoyed just six years on the throne.

The Ramesseum, meanwhile, with its extensive array of granaries and storage magazines, remained an important economic institution throughout the twentieth dynasty and served as the main administrative center for western Thebes until the collapse of central government at the end of the reign of Ramesses XI. During a labor dispute in the reign of Ramesses III, prompted by the late payment of wages to the necropolis workers—the machinery of government was too preoccupied with the pharaoh's impending jubilee celebrations, the first in Egypt since the reign of Ramesses II—it was to the Ramesseum that the disgruntled workmen marched, their flaming torches lighting up the night sky, to demand a resolution of their grievances.[5] They knew only too well that supplies of grain, precious metals, and other goods of value were stored behind the Ramesseum's imposing enclosure wall, even if the stone temple at its heart had begun to be recycled for new royal monuments.

Ramesses II's posthumous reputation not only survived the end of the twentieth dynasty, it positively prospered in the fractious and divided centuries that followed. His reign came to be seen as a golden age—quite possibly Egypt's last—to which successive generations looked back with nostalgia, and which each succeeding pharaoh, more in hope than in expectation, sought to recapture.[6] In the three centuries or so of political turmoil that comprised the twenty-first to twenty-fifth dynasties—known collectively to Egyptologists as the Third Intermediate Period—a dozen kings chose variants of Usermaatra as their throne name. (It seems to have become synonymous with "pharaoh," much as "Caesar" later came to stand for "emperor.")[7] Most reigned for less than a decade. Only one, Shoshenq III of the twenty-second dynasty (who chose the throne name Usermaatra-setepenra), came anywhere close to Ramesses II's record, exercising power for nearly four decades. But these reigns were, at best, a dim afterglow of Ramesside glory, never approaching the real thing.

The Ramesseum was finally abandoned as a religious and economic powerhouse, its granaries reused as funerary chapels. The city of Per-Ramesses, too, was deserted, its location rendered redundant when the Pelusiac branch of the Nile silted up and the river permanently changed its course. Its abundant statuary, obelisks, and stone architecture were systematically stripped and reused to build and adorn new dynastic capitals at Tanis and Bubastis. Although the city of Per-Ramesses disappeared, its memory lingered on, and not only in the minds of the Egyptians: three of the first five books of the Hebrew Bible, compiled during and immediately after the Babylonian exile of the Jews in the sixth century B.C., refer to the land or city of "Rameses": "And Joseph placed his father and his brethren, and gave them a possession in the land of Egypt, in the best of the land, in the land of Rameses, as Pharaoh had commanded."[8]

Even as late as the fourth century B.C., nine hundred years after Ramesses' death, exotic details of his long and eventful reign were still current in folk memory. A stela of the period, which was set up inside a shrine next to the temple of Khonsu within the great temple enclosure at Karnak, is inscribed with a remarkable tale set in the far-off days of Ramesses II. The Bentresh Stela, as it is known today, tells how the king traveled to the land of Naharin (Mesopotamia), where he received in marriage the eldest daughter of the prince of Bakhtan (Bactria).[9] The pharaoh named her Neferura. This part of the story seems to merge memories of Ramesses' marriage to a Hittite princess (who was given the Egyptian name Maathor-Neferura), and the more recent marriage of Alexander the Great—who as pharaoh of Egypt took the suitably Ramesside throne name Setepenra-meryamun—to the Bactrian princess Rhoxane. The tale goes on to recount how, some years later, the Egyptian ruler learned that Neferura's younger sister, Bentresh, had fallen ill. He sent a scribe and sage named Djehutyemheb to heal her, in an episode that recalls the sending of a physician by Ramesses II to the court of the Hittite king. The rest of the story is pure myth: Djehutyemheb fails in his task, because Bentresh is possessed by a demon. The prince of Bakhtan therefore asks Ramesses to send a divine statue, which he duly does. The statue of Khonsu-the-provider expels the demon and cures the princess; but her father keeps the statue, impressed by its power. After three years and nine months, the prince has a dream in which he sees the god transform into a golden falcon, leave his shrine, and fly back to Egypt. On awakening, the prince realizes that he must let the god go, and sends the statue back to Ramesses.

The tale of Ramesses and the Bactrian princess was written by priests of Khonsu to glorify their particular deity; as such, it was probably not well known beyond a narrow theological circle. By contrast, in the Ptolemaic and Roman periods the canon of popular literature included two narratives that featured Prince Khaemwaset, still remembered a millennium after his death as sem-priest and scholar, but now also attributed with magical powers.[10] In the first story of the so-called Setna-Khaemwaset Cycle, the prince encounters the spirit of a fellow magician from Egypt's remote past in an ancient tomb (echoes of the historic Khaemwaset's interest in antiquity); while in the second story reflections on the afterlife — perhaps recalling Khaemwaset's career as high priest of Ptah — weave together Greek and Egyptian themes in ways that presage early Christian theology. Through oral tradition and memory, the events and principal characters of Ramesses II's reign had a unique and lasting influence on subsequent generations, literatures, and religions.

OZYMANDIAS

Such was the renown of Ramesses and his monuments that the historians of the Persian, Ptolemaic, and Roman periods could not fail to mention him in their writings, even if knowledge of his true identity and the details of his reign were hazy. In the fifth century B.C., Herodotus, "the father of history," recounted the tales he had heard about "Rhampsinitus" and claimed to have seen the king's buildings at Memphis. Two centuries later, Manetho — an Egyptian priest and scholar who had access to ancient king lists and devised the system of dynasties still used by Egyptologists today — wrote of a king called either Rapsakes or (more accurately) Ramesses-miamun. The Roman authors Pliny and Tacitus mentioned "Rhameseis" and "Rhamses," respectively, and seem to have been the last scholars before modern times to have remembered the pharaoh's name correctly. Most influential, however, in terms of later antiquarian interest in the life and achievements of Ramesses II was the first-century B.C. Greek historian Diodorus Siculus. He knew the name "Remphis," but when writing of the temple, statues, and battle scenes of the Ramesseum referred to the building as the "Tomb of Osymandyas" — this being a garbled Greek rendering of the pharaoh's throne name, Usermaatra. Thus the legend of Ozymandias, king of kings, was born.[11]

The modern history of Egyptology, and of the rediscovery of Ramesses, began with the Napoleonic expedition to Egypt in 1798. In the plans of Thebes produced by Bonaparte's savants, the Ramesseum was still labeled, following Diodorus Siculus, "Tombeau d'Osymandyas," but the authors noted that other travelers had dubbed it the "Palais de Memnon." Members of the expedition also noted the presence in the temple's second court of a massive

Ozymandias: The fallen colossus of Ramesses in the Ramesseum,
the king's memorial temple at Thebes (author photo).

bust of the pharaoh, with a second royal head nearby, and fragments of a truly gargantuan colossus lying prone on the sand. Napoleon took a keen interest in acquiring antiquities for display in
the French capital, and an attempt was made to remove the larger
and more spectacular of the two busts, which was cut from a single block of stone and measured more than 8 feet high and 6½ feet

wide. But at 7¼ tons, the bust was simply too heavy, and the attempt was abandoned. It was not until Napoleon's defeat at Waterloo in 1815, and the subsequent determination by the British to counter French cultural hegemony in Egypt, that a serious plan was hatched to seize the bust of Ozymandias — or the "Younger Memnon," as it was better known — as the ultimate prize and symbol of European supremacy.[12]

The story of Ramesses' journey from his memorial temple on the west bank of the Nile to the banks of the Thames involves four extraordinary characters of early nineteenth-century antiquarianism. The first was Henry Salt, who in April 1816 arrived in Cairo as the British government's new consul-general in Egypt. He would devote most of the next decade to collecting antiquities, not only for the British Museum but also to sell at a profit to supplement his meager diplomatic salary. The second was a Swiss explorer, Johann Ludwig Burckhardt, who had studied Arabic at Cambridge, traveled extensively in the Middle East, discovered Petra in 1812, and later that year settled in Cairo, living as a Muslim under the name Sheikh Ibrahim ibn Abdullah. Burckhardt was fascinated by Egypt's antiquities in general, and by the Younger Memnon in particular. As a later account noted: "Mr. Burckhardt had for a long time premeditated the removal of the colossal head, or rather bust, known by the name of Young Memnon, to England, and had often endeavored to persuade the Bashaw [Pasha] to send it as a present to the Prince Regent; but as it must have appeared to a Turk too trifling an article to send to so great a personage, no steps were taken for this purpose."[13] Burckhardt was supported in his scheme by another traveler and antiquarian, William John Bankes, who had come to Egypt in 1815. He was an avid collector of antiquities, and the idea of transporting the Younger Memnon to England to stand as the centerpiece of the British Museum greatly appealed to him. Indeed, he had given it a try himself, taking ropes and pulleys to the Ramesseum, but had given up, defeated by the statue's utter immovability. Together, Burckhardt and Bankes pressed their case with the newly arrived British consul-general, Salt. The missing element was someone bold – or foolish – enough to attempt the task of removing the colossal head from its temple and transporting it to the Nile.

Enter the fourth, and pivotal, character in the story, an Italian circus strongman turned hydraulic engineer named Giovanni Battista Belzoni. Belzoni had been born into poverty in Padua and moved to Rome as a teenager, intent upon a career in holy orders. Forced to leave the city by Napoleon's invasion in 1798, Belzoni had wandered around Europe for four years as a peddler, before arriving in London in 1802. There he put his extraordinary physical stature to good use, taking to the stage as a weightlifter (billed, successively, as "the Patagonian Sampson," "the French Hercules," and "the Great Belzoni"). After a decade in the theater, he sought new adventures and journeyed to Malta and thence to Egypt, at the invitation of the country's ruler, Muhammad Ali Pasha. (Belzoni had convinced the Pasha's agent that a background in theatrical hydraulics could be applied equally successfully to improving Egypt's irrigation system.) By this extraordinary combination of circumstances, Belzoni arrived in Cairo just as Salt was considering the proposal from Burckhardt and Bankes. The Italian giant – doughty, fearless, and uncannily experienced in moving heavy objects – presented the perfect solution. On June 28, 1816, Salt wrote in a letter: "Mr. Belzoni is requested to prepare the necessary implements, at Boolak [Bulaq], for the purpose of raising the head of the statue of the younger Memnon, and carrying it down the Nile."[14] Belzoni accepted the commission and set off for Thebes.

On arrival, he recruited eighty local Arab men, and they began work on July 27.

Within a week, the colossal head had been dragged nearly four hundred yards. Another nine days later, on August 12, it had reached the bank of the Nile. The Younger Memnon's journey downstream to Cairo took twenty-four days, and the statue eventually docked at the port of Bulaq on December 15. After a break for the Christmas and New Year festivities, the torso embarked on a second river journey, arriving at the port of Rosetta, at the mouth of the Nile, on January 10, 1817. There it stayed in quarantine for nine months, while the British authorities pondered how on earth to transport it to London. Eventually, on October 17, 1817, Henry Salt reported that the head had been embarked on the transport ship *Nearchus* and was bound for Malta. There it was transferred to a Royal Navy storeship, HMS *Weymouth,* for the final journey to England. Throughout the torso's long voyage from Luxor to London, news of its progress was eagerly covered by the European press.

One man who took a particular interest in the statue's journey was the poet Percy Bysshe Shelley, who was an avid reader of travelers' tales from "oriental" lands. At Christmas 1817, he challenged the banker and political writer Horace Smith — a member of Shelley's literary circle who was staying with the poet and his wife over the festive season — to write a sonnet on the subject, while he would do the same. The starting point for their poetic efforts was the description of the "tomb of Osymandyas" in the writings of Diodorus Siculus: "King of Kings am I, Osymandyas. If anyone would know how great I am and where I lie, let him surpass one of my works."[15] Shelley's sonnet, titled simply "Ozymandias," was published on January 11, 1818, as the Younger Memnon was making its way up the English Channel. It remains the most famous meditation in the English language on the fragility of human power:

> I met a traveller from an antique land
> Who said: "Two vast and trunkless legs of stone
> Stand in the desert. Near them on the sand,
> Half sunk, a shattered visage lies, whose frown
> And wrinkled lip and sneer of cold command
> Tell that its sculptor well those passions read
> Which yet survive, stamped on these lifeless things,
> The hand that mocked them and the heart that fed.
> And on the pedestal these words appear:
> 'My name is Ozymandias, king of kings:
> Look on my works, ye mighty, and despair!'
> Nothing beside remains. Round the decay
> Of that colossal wreck, boundless and bare,
> The lone and level sands stretch far away."

Smith's attempt was published three weeks later, also under the title "Ozymandias":

> In Egypt's sandy silence, all alone,
> Stands a gigantic Leg, which far off throws
> The only shadow that the Desert knows: —
> "I am great OZYMANDIAS," saith the stone,
> "The King of Kings; this mighty City shows
> The wonders of my hand." —The City's gone, —
> Naught but the Leg remaining to disclose
> The site of this forgotten Babylon.

We wonder, — and some Hunter may express
Wonder like ours, when thro' the wilderness
Where London stood, holding the Wolf in chace,
He meets some fragment huge, and stops to guess
What powerful but unrecorded race
Once dwelt in that annihilated place.

In later collections, in deference to his friend — and, it must be said, to much the finer poem — Smith retitled his effort, somewhat clumsily, "On a Stupendous Leg of Granite, Discovered Standing by Itself in the Deserts of Egypt, with the Inscription Inserted Below." Unlike Shelley's sonnet, Smith's ode to Ramesside royalty languishes in obscurity.

Eventually, in March 1818, the *Weymouth* anchored in the Thames, and the Foreign Office and Admiralty were able, finally, to notify the British Museum that its prize had arrived. A contemporary periodical, the *Quarterly Review,* had described it as "without doubt the finest specimen of ancient Egyptian sculpture which has yet been discovered."[16] The director of the British Museum, Joseph Banks, concurred, lauding it as "a chef d'oeuvre of Egyptian sculpture."[17] With its acquisition, the museum became "the first repository in the world of Egyptian art and antiquity."[18] The Younger Memnon (inventory number EA19 in the museum's catalogue of Egyptian antiquities) went on permanent display toward the end of 1818. One of its early admirers was Shelley's friend and fellow poet John Keats. Within four years, the statue became perhaps the first ancient Egyptian artifact to be studied at length in a scientific publication, not merely as a trophy but as an art historical object in its own right.[19]

Although Burckhardt and Belzoni are today best remembered

for their parts in the transport of the Younger Memnon to London, they were also pivotal figures in the rediscovery and exploration of another of Ramesses II's surviving monuments—arguably the greatest of all the pharaoh's artistic and architectural achievements, Abu Simbel. Like the "tomb of Ozymandias" at Thebes, Ramesses' great rock-cut temples in Nubia had attracted the attention of travelers from the classical world. In the sixth century B.C., mercenaries from Caria, Ionia, and Phoenicia serving in the army of Pharaoh Psamtek II in his campaign against the Kushites had carved their names just below the knee of the southern colossus next to the entrance of the Great Temple, indicating that sand was already starting to bury the monument. By the time Burckhardt visited the site in March 1813—becoming the first European in modern times to do so—the temple had been further engulfed. Belzoni was next to take a keen interest in Abu Simbel, visiting in 1817 (no doubt at Burkhardt's suggestion) as his reward for successfully man-handling the Younger Memnon to the banks of the Nile. His first impression was of a great edifice fast disappearing under the encroaching dunes: "On my approaching the temple, the hope that I had formed of opening its entrance vanished at once; for the amazing accumulation of sand was such, that it appeared an impossibility ever to reach the door."[20] Undeterred, he returned with armies of local workmen and finally succeeded in entering the temple—possibly the first person to do so since pharaonic times—later that year.[21] It was not until 1844 that the Prussian scholar Richard Lepsius managed to copy the reliefs inside and outside the temple, and a full clearance was not achieved until 1869, in a colossal undertaking led by the Frenchman (and first director of the Egyptian Antiquities Service) Auguste Mariette.

Abu Simbel also played a key, if now largely forgotten, role in the breakthrough that marked the birth of Egyptology as a scientific discipline: the decipherment of hieroglyphic script by Jean-François Champollion in 1822. By identifying the names of two Ptolemaic rulers, Ptolemy and Cleopatra, in the Greek and hieroglyphic sections of the bilingual Rosetta Stone (discovered by the Napoleonic expedition in 1801), and on an obelisk belonging to William Bankes (which he had transported from the island of Philae to his English country seat at Kingston Lacy), Champollion correctly deduced the phonetic value of a number of hieroglyphic signs. But his system had up to that point proved its accuracy only when applied to the Greek and Latin names of Egypt's Ptolemaic and Roman rulers. There remained the distressing possibility that the use of a hieroglyphic "alphabet" might have been an invention of the Ptolemies, introduced to facilitate the spelling of "foreign" names, and not a true indication of how the script worked when applied to the indigenous Egyptian language. Then, on the morning of September 14, 1822, Champollion received copies of some of the reliefs at Abu Simbel; they had been made by a fellow Frenchman, Jean-Nicolas Hugot, who had recently visited Egypt with Bankes. In the royal cartouches that occurred over and over again in inscriptions from the temple, Champollion recognized the symbol of the sun (re in the Coptic language), followed by three signs, the last two of which were the symbol that he had already identified as the letter S. From his knowledge of Manetho, Champollion knew of the existence of several kings of the nineteenth and twentieth dynasties named Ramesses; the name also occurred in the Bible. "Thus at last Champollion was assured that the alphabetic characters of his Ptolemaic cartouches were used similarly in distant Pharaonic times. . . . The path to success in the interpretation of the ancient Egyptian records was now clearly defined."[22] He announced his breakthrough in his now famous *Lettre à M. Dacier*, which was read aloud at the Académie des Inscriptions et Belles-Lettres in Paris on September 27, 1822.

RAMESSES UNWRAPPED

The decipherment of hieroglyphics not only opened up the wonders of ancient Egypt to scientific inquiry, it also paved the way for the Nile Valley and its monuments to become tourist attractions—especially for well-heeled visitors from Europe and America seeking to escape the winter in their home countries. Within a few decades of Champollion's breakthrough, scores of *dahabiyas* (houseboats) were transporting parties of sightseers up the Nile each season, from the port of Bulaq (in modern Cairo) to the First Cataract at Aswan—and, for the more adventurous traveler, on to Wadi Halfa at the border between Egypt and Sudan. Most tourists came for the warm, dry climate and the exotic thrill of the "Orient" (observed, at a safe distance, from their comfortably appointed cabins). A few, however, developed a genuine interest in Egypt's pharaonic monuments. Among the many spectacular ruins visited on a typical trip up the Nile, the monuments of Ramesses II loomed large. Before departing Bulaq, a visitor might be taken to see the king's prone colossus at Memphis. Sailing south, boats would pass the ruins of Sheikh Ibada, with the temple of Ramesses visible from the river. On arrival at Luxor, dahabiyas usually moored up next to the temple, dominated by Ramesses' great pylon, statues, and obelisk. No excursion to the west bank would be complete without a visit to the Ramesseum, its first court still dominated by the fallen colossus of Ozymandias. And the undoubted highlight of any Nile cruise was Abu Simbel, "the noblest monument of antiquity that is to be found on the banks of the Nile."[23]

The temples of Abu Simbel made an immediate and lasting impression on everyone who saw them. For most tourists, the great rock-hewn edifices provided an unforgettable culmination to their Nile journey, an encounter with which to regale friends and family back home. But for one tourist traveling up the Nile in the winter of 1873–1874, the visit to Abu Simbel proved a life-changing experience and a decisive moment in the history of Egyptology. The individual in question was a successful Victorian novelist by the name of Amelia Edwards. Her decision to go up the Nile was taken on a whim, when poor weather in Europe forced a last-minute change in her holiday plans. But the sheer scale, sophistication, and antiquity of Egypt's pharaonic monuments, especially those at Abu Simbel, struck a chord with Edwards's romantic sensibilities. She fell in love not just with the Nile Valley in general but with Ramesses II in particular.

Edwards's hugely influential account of her trip, *A Thousand Miles up the Nile,* devoted an entire chapter to "Rameses the Great," whom she lauded as "the central figure of Egyptian history." Paraphrasing Malvolio in Shakespeare's *Twelfth Night,* Edwards described Ramesses thus: "He was born to greatness; he achieved greatness; and he had borrowed greatness thrust upon him." In her inimitable style, she noted the sheer ubiquity of his monuments along the length and breadth of the Nile Valley:

> The interest that one takes in Rameses II begins at Memphis, and goes on increasing all the way up the river. It is a purely living, a purely personal interest; such as one feels in Athens for Pericles, or in Florence for Lorenzo the Magnificent. Other Pharaohs but languidly affect the imagination. Thothmes [Thutmose] and Amenhotep are to us as Darius

or Artaxerxes — shadows that come and go in the distance. But with the second Rameses we are on terms of respectful intimacy. We seem to know the man — to feel his presence — to hear his name in the air. His features are as familiar to us as those of Henry the Eighth or Louis the Fourteenth. His cartouches meet us at every turn. Even to those who do not read the hieroglyphic character, those well-known signs convey, by sheer force of association, the name and style of Rameses, beloved of Amen.

She went farther, describing Ramesses as a "popular hero," as if he were the central character in one of her romantic novels.[24] Applying such characterization to individuals from Egyptian antiquity was something new, and Edwards's readers found its immediacy compelling. Through her writing, Ramesses II emerged from history as a full-fledged personality in his own right.

During the preparation of *A Thousand Miles up the Nile*, Edwards combined her own notes with the latest Egyptological research, and was thus able — unlike any previous lay writer on Egypt — to introduce her readers to the historical details of Ramesses' reign: his proclamation as heir apparent (based on a translation of the Great Dedicatory Inscription at Abydos), the Battle of Kadesh, the peace treaty with the Hittites, and the first Hittite marriage. Edwards confidently identified Ramesses as the pharaoh of the Israelite captivity, following the received wisdom of the time. Above all, she noted his overriding passion for building.

If Ramesses is the dominant figure of Edwards's book, then his chef d'oeuvre, Abu Simbel, is the monument around which her narrative pivots. In her words, the Nubian site was "the most stupendous historical record ever transmitted from the past to the present." The dark, mysterious interior of the Great Temple appealed to her imagination:

It is a wonderful place to be alone in—a place in which the very darkness and silence are old, and in which Time himself seems to have fallen asleep. Wandering to and fro among these sculptured halls, like a shade among shadows, one seems to have left the world behind; to have done with the teachings of the present; to belong one's self to the past. The very Gods assert their ancient influence over those who question them in solitude. Seen in the fast-deepening gloom of evening, they look instinct with supernatural life. There were times when I should scarcely have been surprised to hear them speak—to see them rise from their painted thrones and come down from the walls. There were times when I felt I believed in them.

The four colossal statues of Ramesses himself fronting the facade of the Great Temple made the greatest impression: "Every morning I saw those awful brethren pass from death to life, from life to sculptured stone. I brought myself almost to believe at last that there must sooner or later come some one sunrise when the ancient chasm would snap asunder, and the giants must arise and speak." Edwards thought she detected "a godlike serenity, an almost superhuman pride, and immutable will," declaring of Ramesses: "He has learned to believe his prowess irresistible, and himself almost divine. If he now raised his arm to slay, it would be with the stern placidity of a destroying angel."[25]

The acclaim that greeted the publication of *A Thousand Miles up the Nile* in 1877 and the book's enduring popularity had two immediate effects. The first was to raise the profile of Ramesses II in the public consciousness as the greatest pharaoh of them all, a position he has held ever since—albeit with some competition from the boy-king Tutankhamun. The second, and the true goal of Edwards's publication, was to rally support for her new mission: to encourage the study and preservation of Egypt's ancient patrimony before it was lost forever. On her journey up the Nile, wonder at the pharaonic monuments had been matched by horror at their wanton destruction. In nineteenth-century Egypt's headlong rush toward modernization, temples that had stood largely untouched for millennia were being torn down to feed lime kilns, build barrages, or clear land for cultivation. Edwards was appalled at the pace of demolition, and she wrote her book as a call to action. To great dramatic effect, she juxtaposed her awestruck description of Abu Simbel with an account of the obliteration of other ancient sites. Her subsequent indefatigable campaigning and fundraising led to the establishment of the Egypt Exploration Fund (today the Egypt Exploration Society), which remains among her greatest legacies to Egyptology.

Due to the pace of Egyptological discoveries during the last quarter of the nineteenth century, the second edition of Edwards's book, published in 1889, was able to incorporate a wealth of new evidence about Ramesses II. Indeed, no longer did historians have to rely on the pharaoh's monuments to discern something of his character: they could now look upon the face of the king himself. For in 1881, Theban villagers had discovered a cache of royal and noble mummies — more than fifty in total — in a tomb high in the cliffs behind the Valley of the Kings. One of the bodies, placed in an ordinary wooden coffin, was carefully labeled as that of the great Ramesses. According to the hieroglyphic inscription, the mummy had undergone something of an ordeal before being reinterred. Priests had first removed it from Ramesses' tomb in the Valley of the Kings to thwart looters. Initially, the body was transferred to a holding area inside the tomb of Ahmose-Inhapy, a royal princess of the early eighteenth dynasty. Then, three days later, together with a host of other royal mummies, it was moved to the tomb of the twenty-first-dynasty high priest of Amun, Pinedjem II, in the hills between Deir el-Bahri and the Valley of the Kings.

Five years after the discovery of the "royal cache," on June 1, 1886, the mummy of Ramesses II (given the inventory number 5233) was unwrapped at the Egyptian Museum in Bulaq under the supervision of the French director-general of Egyptian antiquities, Gaston Maspero, and in the presence of the modern ruler of Egypt, Khedive Tewfiq. Maspero's account, issued in an official report two days later, bears quoting at length, providing as it does the most detailed account published to that date of the postmortem treatment of an Egyptian pharaoh:

> The first wrapping was removed, and there was successively discovered a band of stuff 20 centimètres in width rolled round the body; then a second winding sheet sewn up and kept in place by narrow bands placed at some distance apart; then two thicknesses of small bandages; and then a piece of fine linen reaching from the head to the feet. A figure representing the Goddess Nut, one métre [*sic*] in length, is drawn upon this piece of linen, in red and white, as prescribed by ritual. . . . Under this amulet there was found another bandage; then a layer of pieces of linen folded in squares and spotted with the bituminous matter used by the embalmers. This last covering removed, Rameses II. appeared. The head is long, and small in proportion to the body. The top of the skull is quite bare. On the temples there are a few sparse hairs, but at the poll the hair is quite thick, forming smooth, straight locks about five centimétres in length. White at the time of death, they have been dyed a light yellow by the spices used in embalment. The forehead is low and narrow; the brow-ridge prominent; the eyebrows are thick and white; the eyes are small and close together; the nose is long, thin, hooked like the noses of the Bourbons, and slightly crushed

at the tip by the pressure of the bandages. The temples are sunken; the cheekbones are very prominent; the ears round, standing far out from the head, and pierced like those of a woman for the wearing of earrings. The jawbone is massive and strong; the chin very prominent; the mouth small but thick lipped, and full of some kind of black paste. This paste[,] being partly cut away with a scissors, disclosed some much worn and very brittle teeth, which, moreover, are white and well preserved. The moustache and beard are thin. They seem to have been kept shaven during life, but were probably allowed to grow during the king's last illness. . . . The hairs are white like those of the head and eyebrows, but are harsh and bristly, and from two to three millimètres in length. The skin is of earthy brown splotched with black. Finally, it may be said the face of the mummy gives a fair idea of the face of the living King. The expression is unintellectual, perhaps slightly animal; but even under the somewhat grotesque disguise of mummification, there is plainly to be seen an air of sovereign majesty, of resolve, and of pride.

The whole process of unwrapping took less than fifteen minutes. In summary, concluded Maspero, "The corpse is that of an old man, but a vigorous and robust old man."[26]

The subsequent history of Ramesses' mummy is every bit as dramatic as his initial reburial and rediscovery. In 1975, a French doctor, Maurice Bucaille, noticed that the body, kept under inadequate conditions at the Egyptian Museum in Cairo's polluted city center, was deteriorating rapidly. At the request of the French government, it was flown to Paris for scientific study and treatment.[27] The international media, always eager for a sensational story concerning ancient Egypt, concocted a false report that the pharaoh had been issued with an Egyptian passport, which gave his occupation as "King (deceased)." What is true is that the mummy was greeted on arrival at Paris's Le Bourget airport in September the following year with full military honors before being taken to the Musée de l'Homme for examination. There, in a special, sterile room, it was inspected by the chief forensic scientist at the Criminal Identification Laboratory, Pierre-Fernand Ceccaldi, who revealed pierced ears (to accommodate heavy gold earrings), old fractures, and battle wounds. The great pharaoh, it transpired, had suffered in old age from poor circulation, arthritis, ankylosing spondilitis, and a painful abscess in his jaw. Pollen in the unguents used in mummification showed conclusively that the process had been carried out in the Delta, not in the Nile Valley.

Perhaps most interesting of all, examination of Ramesses' head showed that he had been fair-skinned with wavy ginger hair. Indeed, it is likely that he came from a family of redheads. This is intriguing on two counts: first, because in ancient Egypt the color red was associated with the god Seth, who was clearly regarded by the nineteenth-dynasty royal family as its patron deity; second, because fair skin and red hair, though not unknown, would have been uncommon in ancient Egypt, as they are in Egypt today, and would have set the Ramesside royal family apart from most of their subjects. Standing five feet, eight inches, tall, with an aquiline nose, strong jaw, and bright red hair, the youthful Ramesses II must have cut a striking, not to say exotic, figure. Perhaps Amelia Edwards had been right after all when she averred that "Rameses the Great . . . must have been one of the handsomest men, not only of his day, but of all history."[28]

After being irradiated to eliminate fungal infections and an infestation of insects, the body of Ramesses II was finally returned to Cairo in May 1977, his casket draped in a mantle of lapis lazuli-colored velvet, embroidered in gold thread with the heraldic emblems of Upper and Lower Egypt, sewn by the *tapissiers* of the Louvre. On April 3, 2021, in a procession of eighteen kings and

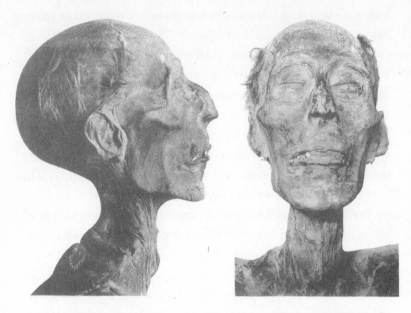

Dignity in death: The head of Ramesses' well-preserved mummy (G. Elliot Smith, *The Royal Mummies* [Cairo: Institut français d'archéologie orientale, 1912], plate XLIV).

four queens dubbed "the Pharaohs' Golden Parade," it was moved in a special float from the Egyptian Museum in the center of the city to the new National Museum of Egyptian Civilization in the Fustat district of Old Cairo. Whether or not it will finally be allowed to rest in peace remains an open question.[29]

A PHARAOH FOR ALL TIME

The interest in Ramesses II, kindled by the transport of the Younger Memnon to London, heightened by Edwards's hagiographic writings, and sustained by modern science, has made him perhaps the best known of all ancient Egyptian kings. He has certainly had more influence than any other ruler of the Nile Valley on the modern reception of ancient Egypt. Because of the vast number of his monuments, commentators have felt emboldened, if not compelled, to speculate on his character. In doing so, they have inevitably reflected the mores, standards, and anxieties of their own age. In mid-nineteenth-century Prussia, for example, the scholar Baron von Bunsen called Ramesses "an unbridled despot, who took advantage of a reign of almost unparalleled length, and of the acquisitions of his father and ancestors, in order to torment his own subjects and strangers to the utmost of his power."[30] A century later, in the aftermath of the Second World War, the American Egyptologist William Hayes was equally scathing, castigating the pharaoh of Kadesh as "a brash young man . . . not overburdened with intelligence and singularly lacking in taste" who nonetheless demonstrated "tremendous energy and personal magnetism."[31] In our own time, we have a deeply conflicted attitude toward megalomaniac rulers: some of us thrill at their audacity and ambition while others recoil at their despotism and vanity.

Although pen portraits of figures from ancient history strike the modern scholar as quaint and unscientific, they are not necessarily wrong. We instinctively recognize traits such as charisma in our modern leaders (for good or ill) yet hesitate to ascribe them to the leaders of the past. The more remote the civilization in time and space from our own, the less confident we feel in describing its prominent figures as real people. A biography of Napoleon would certainly probe his personality traits, but an account of the life of Alexander the Great might be more circumspect. Yet human nature is a constant: the same hopes, fears, passions, and insecurities that motivate politicians and despots of the twenty-first century A.D. are likely to have molded their predecessors of the thirteenth century B.C. The leading expert on nineteenth-dynasty Egypt, Kenneth Kitchen, was undoubtedly correct when he cautioned, "The deeds and attitudes of a Ramesses II cannot just be crudely measured off against our own supposed social values, as simply boastful or megalomania; they must be compared with what were the norms and ideas in *his* culture, not ours."[32] Yet there were surely underlying character traits — as unfashionable as it is today to seek to discern them — that led Ramesses to reign as he did, that enabled him (in contrast, say, to his father or son) to leave an indelible impression on his own and subsequent ages. Like contemporary despots, Ramesses was at once bombastic and thin-skinned. He claimed to command the natural world yet remained ever-conscious of his nonroyal origins. Something of his true character reveals itself in his correspondence with the Hittite royal family: overbearing and demanding, yet with flashes of caustic wit.

To take another aspect of his reign, the status given to Nefertari at Abu Simbel, while undoubtedly serving an ideological purpose, cannot be dismissed as motivated solely by the exigencies of divine kingship. Seti I gave no such prominence on his monuments to his queen, nor did Ramesses III (who, as we have seen, consciously modeled himself in many ways on his predecessor and namesake). A twenty-first-century "objective" interpretation of Ramesses II's architectural masterpiece would point to the precedent set by Amenhotep III (many of whose statues Ramesses usurped) in dedicating an entire Nubian temple to his chief consort. A more romantic, Victorian interpretation discerned a different motive:

> We see, at all events, that Rameses and Nefertari desired to leave behind them an imperishable record of the affection which united them on earth, and which they hoped would reunite them in Amenti [the West]. What more do we need to know? We see that the Queen was fair; that

the King was in his prime. We divine the rest; and the poetry of the place at all events is ours. Even in these barren solitudes there is wafted to us a breath from the shores of old romance. We feel that Love once passed this way, and that the ground is still hallowed where he trod.[33]

The truth probably lies somewhere between the two. The essential point remains: Ramesses II, as we can see from his mummified remains, was a real person. He suffered from identifiably human frailties, and he must have been influenced — as we all are — by recognizably human emotions.

While modern Egyptological scholarship prefers to steer clear of such topics, film and literature have embraced them with gusto. Hollywood early on recognized the appeal of ancient Egypt, especially to the genre of horror movies, and one of the first such films was *La momie du roi* (The Mummy of the King Rameses), released in 1909. In a different vein, Cecil B. DeMille's 1956 classic *The Ten Commandments* starred Yul Brynner as Ramesses II, portraying the pharaoh as a vengeful tyrant, shaped by jealousy of his father's affection for Moses (who, in the film, is Ramesses' adopted brother). The same trope of sibling rivalry provided the narrative force for the animated film *The Prince of Egypt* (1998), and Ramesses was a central character in the 2014 film *Exodus: Gods and Kings*. For over a century, the pharaoh has proved good box-office material. Novelists, too, have found much to inspire them in the story — real or imagined — of Ramesses II. Norman Mailer's *Ancient Evenings* (1983) presented a retrospective of the pharaoh's life through the voices of Egyptians living 150 years later, in the reign of Ramesses IX. The exotic culture of ancient Egypt provided Mailer with rich material with which to indulge his interests in mythology and sexuality. At the other end of the literary spectrum, the immensely successful Ramses series of five historical novels by Christian Jacq takes the known details of the pharaoh's reign (Jacq holds a doctorate in Egyptian studies from the Sorbonne) and weaves them into an epic tale of love and deceit, magic and murder.[34]

Indeed, the French — inspired, perhaps, by their role in the scientific examination of Ramesses' mummy in 1886 and again in 1976, or perhaps by the pharaoh's distinctly Gallic profile — have taken Ramesses to their heart. His tomb, partially cleared in the 1810s by the Englishman Henry Salt, mapped in the 1840s by the Prussian Richard Lepsius, and excavated in the 1910s under the patronage of the American Theodore Davis (and the British aristocrat Lord Carnarvon), had been long neglected until a French expedition resumed careful study of its surviving art and architecture in 1991. A multidisciplinary team continues its work, revealing surprising new details from a site long since thought to have given up all its secrets.

International recognition of the cultural importance of Ramesses' legacy peaked in the late 1960s, with the UNESCO campaign to rescue the temples of Abu Simbel from flooding following the building of the Aswan High Dam. The salvage operation was an international effort, involving specialists from a host of nations.[35] Many different solutions were proposed, but eventually, for reasons of practicality and cost, and despite outspoken criticism from some archaeologists, it was decided to remove the temples from their original location to higher ground. Over the course of four years, from 1964 to 1968, the two temples were cut up into blocks and re-erected some 213 feet higher up and 590 feet west of their original location, inside an artificial mountain. (The relocation changed the carefully planned alignment of the Great Temple, with the effect that the rising sun now illuminates the sanctuary one day later than in ancient times.) The Egyptian government had first appealed to UNESCO for help in 1959. The then director-general, Vittorio Veronese, knew immediately that the organization had to respond positively. As he noted, "We cannot allow temples like Abu Simbel and Philae, which are veritable gems of ancient art, to disappear; nor can we abandon forever the treasures which lie buried in the sand on sites not yet systematically excavated. Here is an exemplary occasion for demonstrating the international solidarity which Unesco has been striving to make a reality in all domains."[36]

On September 22, 1968, after an operation involving seventeen hundred workers and costing some $36 million, the temples of Abu Simbel were officially reopened. The occasion was marked in many countries with the issue of special commemorative postage stamps, and at Abu Simbel itself with a host of speeches. The chairman of the executive committee of the International Campaign to Save the Monuments of Nubia, Paulo E. de Berrêdo Carneiro, proudly declared, "Posterity will remember with gratitude that, for almost fifteen years now, they have devoted their lives to the service of the God-King," and he confidently asserted, "The architects and scribes of Rameses II could return to Abu Simbel without fear. They would find there the temples dedicated to the glory of their master and of his favorite wife, standing just as they built them. Now, as of old, the rays of the rising sun twice yearly will suffuse with light the statue of the god-king in the depths of his sanctuary."[37]

His remarks were merely the warm-up act. The keynote speech that day was delivered by Veronese's successor as UNESCO director-general, the Frenchman René Maheu, who had taken office in 1962, before the commencement of the project. A professor of philosophy and close friend of Jean-Paul Sartre and Simone de Beauvoir, Maheu was the guiding light behind the rescue of Abu Simbel, for he recognized that the site was not simply one of the greatest relics of ancient Egypt but an irreplaceable part of humanity's shared patrimony. At the rededication ceremony, he addressed his remarks not to the gathered dignitaries, nor to the world's media, but to the spirit of the deceased Ramesses himself: "We have come, O King, to add our labours to yours in order that your quest for eternity may be preserved." Channeling Shelley, Maheu spoke of the king's "vanished pomp," and only four months after the May riots that had shaken his native France to the core, struck a suitably revolutionary tone: "Yet know, O King, that we have been led to you from the many quarters of the earth, not by the memory of your power, nor by fidelity to your purpose or respect for your cults. Since the days of your victories, long buried in the remote past, history has been such a succession of empty triumphs that we no longer believe in empires, we abhor the thought of war. Your certainties concerning life and death are no longer ours."[38]

In his closing peroration, Maheu appealed to Ramesses, eternal guardian of Abu Simbel, to bear witness to future generations: "Tell these men, whom we shall not see, yet for whom in truth we have laboured, how Man, appearing for a moment in his universal aspect, came to this place when the waters threatened to submerge you, and how, cleaving the mountain asunder, he seized your colossi and bore them to the summit of the cliff, replacing everything as you desired, so that you, the son of Ra, once the incarnation of power, its pride and its vanity, may henceforth be a symbol of brotherhood, its generosity and its splendour."[39] Only a French philosopher, perhaps, could have uttered such words.

Looking back on the Nubian salvage effort in its seventieth anniversary year, UNESCO called the rescue of Abu Simbel "the campaign that revolutionized the international approach to safeguarding heritage."[40] It marked a turning point in humanity's care for its own past, and it still ranks as the greatest archaeological rescue effort of all time.

But what of the pharaoh who came to symbolize the entire campaign? Does Ramesses II deserve his appellation "the Great"? We generally apply that epithet to rulers who have distinguished themselves as war leaders (Alexander of Macedon, Alfred of Wessex) or patrons of the arts (Catherine of Russia, Frederick of Prussia). Ramesses II meets both criteria, but in different ways. His active military career was relatively short (the campaigns in Nubia in his fourth and fifth decades amounting to little more than punitive raids). The defining event of his reign, the Battle of Kadesh, was a strategic failure but paved the way for a diplomatic triumph. Egypt never captured the city itself and never regained control of the surrounding province. But the inconclusive battle led to a lasting peace with the Hittites, the first mutual nonaggression pact in history, and a welcome period of stability in the wider Near East.[41] Peace in Syria also allowed Ramesses to concentrate on fortifying his western frontier, something that for decades to come served to safeguard Egypt from invasion when so many other civilizations of the eastern Mediterranean succumbed. Had it not been for Ramesses, pharaonic culture might well have been snuffed out a millennium before Cleopatra handed the keys of Egypt to Rome.

In dynastic terms, too, Ramesses' reign had its successes and failures. As a son, the king lived up to the great expectations that had been placed upon him when he was first recognized as heir apparent. In the opening years of his reign, Ramesses completed his father's monuments and secured the royal family's grip on power. In due course, Ramesses fathered more children than any other pharaoh, before or after him. But his urge to create a dynasty had the unintended consequence of destabilizing the line of succession after his death, when countless royal offspring emerged as contenders for the throne. Merenptah, thirteenth son and eventual successor, was already over sixty years old by the time he acceded. His reign was followed by a series of contested, ephemeral rulers, as one faction, then another, jostled for power. The nineteenth dynasty – created by Ramesses I, consolidated by Seti I, and magnified by Ramesses II – ended not with a bang but with a whimper.

Yet despite – or perhaps because of – the weaknesses of his immediate successors, Ramesses II's own reputation, so carefully honed during his long years on the throne, endured for centuries: three hundred years after his death, dignitaries with no royal blood in their veins still gloried in the title "king's son of Ramesses." He wrote his own history and created his own legend. His propaganda efforts were massive and unrelenting, even by the standards of pharaonic Egypt. The Battle of Kadesh still dominates every account of his reign, as he intended it should. He took the deification of the reigning king to new heights, and toward the end of his reign deliberately blurred the distinction between human and divine kingship. As Amelia Edwards memorably remarked, "The Egyptians would seem, beyond all doubt, to have believed that their King was always, in some sense, divine. They wrote hymns and offered up prayers to him, and regarded him as the living representative of Deity. His princes and ministers habitually addressed him in the language of worship. Even his wives, who ought to have known better, are represented in the performance of acts of religious adoration before him. What wonder, then, if the man so deified believed himself a god?"[42]

It is surely Ramesses' achievements as a self-propagandist, given concrete form through an astonishing architectural legacy, that justify his claim to greatness. He established the classic form of an Egyptian temple and left more monuments as witnesses of his motives and achievements than any other pharaoh. In pursuit of contemporary legitimacy and eternal reputation, he usurped huge numbers of his predecessors' statues and temples, and commissioned more of his own, on a grander scale, than any other king of Egypt. From a new residence city in the far northeastern Delta to a series of eight rock-cut temples in Nubia, no section of the Nile Valley was spared the attentions of Ramesses' architects, builders, and sculptors. From north to south, within the traditional borders of Egypt alone his projects included a string of forts along the Libyan border, significant additions to the temples of Heliopolis and Memphis, new temples at Herakleopolis and Sheikh Ibada, major works in the temple of Seti I and a memorial temple of his own at Abydos, the great hypostyle hall at Karnak, the forecourt of Luxor Temple, the Ramesseum, seven royal tombs (for himself, his chief wives, and his children) in the Valley of the Kings and Valley of the Queens – to mention just the major monuments. Ramesses also directed his patronage toward scores of other sites – such as Buto in the northwestern Delta, the Giza Plateau, and Gebel el-Silsila – which held particular resonance for divine kingship in general or the nineteenth dynasty in particular.[43]

The ubiquity of Ramesses' monuments, combined with the fact that most of them feature the king himself as the defining element of their architecture and decoration, has made him, quite simply, the quintessential pharaoh. If we seek one monarch to stand for the entire line of Egyptian kings, it is to Ramesses – his immortal features rendered in stone to last for millions of years – that our thoughts naturally turn. His colossal statues, looking out serenely from the facade of Luxor Temple and Abu Simbel, or lying in the ruins of Memphis and the Ramesseum, represent the epitome of pharaonic civilization: confident and assertive, magnificent and uncompromising, dedicated to the gods but really all about the king. Ramesses himself is but a blank, pharaoh-shaped canvas, onto which every age — including our own — can project its hopes and fears, its preoccupations and aspirations, its contradictory views of authority and control. If we think we recognize the "frown / And wrinkled lip and sneer of cold command," it is because we are looking in the mirror.

Chronology of Ancient Egypt

All dates are B.C. and approximate before 664.

2950–2575	Early Dynastic Period (First to Third Dynasties)
2575–2125	Old Kingdom (Fourth to Eighth Dynasties)
2125–2010	First Intermediate Period (Ninth/Tenth to Eleventh Dynasties)
2010–1630	Middle Kingdom (Eleventh to Thirteenth Dynasties)
1630–1539	Second Intermediate Period (Fourteenth to Seventeenth Dynasties)
1539–1069	New Kingdom (Eighteenth to Twentieth Dynasties)
1539–1292	Eighteenth Dynasty

1539–1514	Ahmose (I)
1514–1493	Amenhotep I
1493–1481	Thutmose I
1481–1479	Thutmose II
1479–1425	Thutmose III and Hatshepsut, 1473–1458
1426–1400	Amenhotep II
1400–1390	Thutmose IV
1390–1353	Amenhotep III
1353–1336	Amenhotep IV/Akhenaten
1336–1332	Smenkhkara
1332–1322	Tutankhamun
1322–1319	Ay
1319–1292	Horemheb

1292–1190　Nineteenth Dynasty

1292–1290	Ramesses I
1290–1279	Seti I
1279–1213	Ramesses II

	1213–1204	Merenptah
	1204–1198	Seti II (Seti-Merenptah)
	1204–1200	Amenmesse
	1198–1193	Siptah
	1198–1190	Tawosret
1190–1069	Twentieth Dynasty	
	1190–1187	Sethnakht
	1187–1156	Ramesses III
	1156–1150	Ramesses IV
	1150–1145	Ramesses V
	1145–1137	Ramesses VI
	1137–1129	Ramesses VII
	1129–1126	Ramesses VIII
	1126–1108	Ramesses IX
	1108–1099	Ramesses X
	1099–1069	Ramesses XI
1069–664	Third Intermediate Period (Twenty-First to Twenty-Fifth Dynasties)	
664–332	Late Period (Twenty-Sixth to Thirty-First Dynasties)	
332–309	Macedonian Dynasty	
309–30	Ptolemaic Period	

Chronology of
Ramesses II's Life and Reign

All dates B.C. and approximate.

1304	Ramesses born, in the reign of Horemheb
1292	Ramesses' grandfather Paramessu succeeds as Ramesses I
1290	Ramesses' father succeeds as Seti I; Ramesses given titular command of the army
1287	Birth of Ramesses' first son, Amunhirwenemef (Amunhirkhepeshef)
1286	R. participates in military action against Libyan tribes in western Delta
1284	R. participates in military action against Kadesh and Amurru
1281	R. appointed co-regent with his father
1279–1278	Year 1
	R. succeeds as sole pharaoh (May 20, 1279); adopts the throne name Usermaatra
	R. travels to Thebes to bury his father and participate in the Festival of the Sanctuary at Luxor
	R. commissions work on Luxor Temple, Karnak, and the Ramesseum
	R. orders the completion of his father's memorial temple at Qurna
	R. leaves commemorative inscription in sandstone quarries at Gebel el-Silsila
	R. visits Abydos, commences work on his own temple, and adopts sunk relief as the style of his reign
	R. appoints Nebwenenef high priest of Amun
1278–1277	Year 2
	R. erects stela at Aswan, leads Nubian campaign, commissions work at Abu Simbel
	R. amends throne name to Usermaatra-setepenra

1277–1276	Year 3
	R. dedicates new forecourt at Luxor Temple; commissions well for gold miners in Eastern Desert
	R. returns to Memphis to prepare for the first military campaign of his reign
1276–1275	Year 4
	R. leads first Syrian campaign
1275–1274	Year 5
	R. leads second Syrian campaign; Battle of Kadesh, May 1–2, 1274
1273–1272	Year 7
	R. leads campaign through Moab and Edom
1272–1271	Year 8
	R. leads third Syrian campaign and siege of Dapur; erects statue of himself at Dapur
	R. commissions statues for Per-Ramesses, including "Ramesses the god"
1270–1269	Year 10
	R. leads fourth Syrian campaign against Tunip and recaptures Dapur
1264–1263	Year 16
	Apis bull (first of reign) buried at Saqqara, overseen by Prince Khaemwaset
	Palace coup in Hatti deposes Mursili III (Urhiteshup)
1262–1261	Year 18
	Probable flight of Hittite prince Urhiteshup to Egypt
1259–1258	Year 21
	R. concludes peace treaty with the Hittites (November 10, 1259)
	R. begins construction work at Derr
1258–1257	Year 22
	Probable death of queen mother, Tuya
1256–1255	Year 24
	R. inaugurates the temples at Abu Simbel

Probable death of king's great wife Nefertari; Isetnofret becomes the new great wife

1255–1254 Year 25

Crown Prince Amunhirkhepeshef/Sethhirkhepeshef dies; Prince Ramesses declared heir

1250–1249 Year 30

R. celebrates first jubilee

Apis bull (second of reign) buried at Saqqara, overseen by Prince Khaemwaset

1249–1248 Year 31

Probable earthquake at Abu Simbel

1247–1246 Year 33

R. begins construction work at Gerf Hussein

1246–1245 Year 34

R. celebrates second jubilee

Probable death of king's great wife Isetnofret; Bintanat becomes the new great wife

R. marries daughter of Hittite king Hattusili III

1245–1244 Year 35

R. commissions "Blessing of Ptah" inscription

1243–1242 Year 37

R. celebrates third jubilee

1240–1239 Year 40

R. celebrates fourth jubilee

1237–1236 Year 43

R. celebrates fifth jubilee

Probable Apis bull (third of reign) buried at Saqqara

1236–1235 Year 44

Minor campaign in Nubia provides workforce for building Wadi es-Sebua

R. marries second daughter of Hittite king Hattusili III

1235–1234	Year 45
	R. celebrates sixth jubilee
1232–1231	Year 48
	R. celebrates seventh jubilee
1230–1229	Year 50
	Crown Prince Ramesses dies; Prince Khaemwaset declared heir
1228–1227	Year 52
	R. celebrates eighth jubilee
1226–1225	Year 54
	R. celebrates ninth jubilee
1225–1224	Year 55
	Apis bull (fourth of reign) buried at Saqqara in the new underground galleries (the Serapeum)
	Crown Prince Khaemwaset dies; Prince Merenptah declared heir
1223–1222	Year 57
	R. celebrates tenth jubilee
1220–1219	Year 60
	R. celebrates eleventh jubilee
1219–1218	Year 61
	R. celebrates twelfth jubilee
1217–1216	Year 63
	R. celebrates thirteenth jubilee
1213	Year 67
	R. dies at Per-Ramesses, after a reign of sixty-six years and two months; succeeded by Merenptah

Genealogy

*Simplified family tree of the late eighteenth and early nineteenth
dynasties. Reigning monarchs are shown in CAPITALS.
Dotted lines indicate uncertain relationships.*

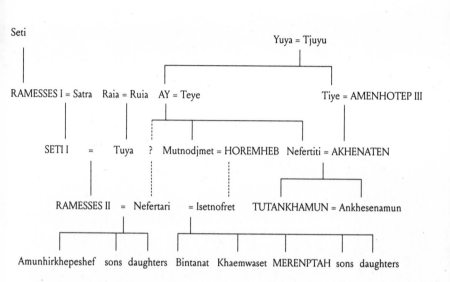

Notes

Unless otherwise stated, all translations from ancient Egyptian texts are mine. Citations to Kitchen, RITA, reference Kitchen, Rames-side Inscriptions Translated and Annotated.

INTRODUCTION

1. A lunar observation from a ship's log, dated to Year 52 of Ramesses II's reign, fixes his accession in one of three years—1304, 1290, or 1279 B.C.; only the third option fits all the known dating evidence from Egypt and Near Eastern sources (see Kitchen, *RITA*, 526).

2. Edwards, *A Thousand Miles*, 257.

3. See Freed, "Akhenaten's Artistic Legacy"; Frood, *Biographical Texts*, 15–25.

4. Notable studies of Ramesses II's reign, all of which speculate on aspects of his personality, include Kitchen, *Pharaoh Triumphant*; Desroches Noblecourt, *Ramsès II*; Menu, *Ramesses the Great*; and Tyldesley, *Ramesses*. For the historical background, see Kitchen, "Ramesses II"; Vandersleyen, *L'Égypte et la Vallée du Nil*, 513–556; and van Dijk, "The Amarna Period and the Later New Kingdom," esp. 288–294.

CHAPTER 1. GREAT EXPECTATIONS

1. Quotations from the coronation inscription and the Edict of Horemheb, respectively. Hieroglyphic editions of nineteenth- and twentieth-dynasty texts are given in Kitchen, *Ramesside Inscriptions*.

2. See Gaballa and Kitchen, "Ramesside Varia I."

3. Dodson and Hilton, *The Complete Royal Families*, 158–175.

4. This was a phrase used frequently in ancient Egyptian texts to describe the prostration required of those seeking supplication.

5. For an overview of the reign of Ramesses I, see Allen, "Ramesses I"; Kitchen, *Pharaoh Triumphant*, 18–20.

6. For an overview of the reign of Seti I and Ramesses' involvement in his father's activities, see Kitchen, *Pharaoh Triumphant*, 20–41.

7. Seti I, first Beth-Shan stela, Year 1.

8. For the Asiatic campaigns of Seti I and Egypt's relations with the Hittites before Ramesses II's accession, see Murnane, *The Road to Kadesh*.

9. Kubban stela; Abydos, Great Dedicatory Inscription.

10. Smith, "Gebel el-Silsila."

11. Seti I, larger Aswan stela, Year 9; see also Habachi, "The Two Rock-Stelae."

12. Ricke, Hughes, and Wente, *The Beit el-Wali Temple;* Kitchen, *RITA,* 111–114; Fletcher-Jones, *Abu Simbel,* 189–192.

13. The Sherden later appear as members of Ramesses II's royal bodyguard at the Battle of Kadesh (Abbas, "The Bodyguard of Ramesses II") and, in the reign of Ramesses III, as part of the enemy coalition dubbed the Sea Peoples. A link has been made on etymological grounds between the Sherden and Sardinia, although the Sherden are likely to have originated in the eastern Mediterranean.

14. Shubert, "Abydos, Osiris Temple of Seti I"; Wegner, "Abydos."

15. Abydos, Great Dedicatory Inscription. For the debate over the nature and length of the co-regency between Seti I and Ramesses II, see Murnane, "The Earlier Reign"; Murnane, *Ancient Egyptian Coregencies;* Vandersleyen, *L'Égypte et la Vallée du Nil,* 510–512.

16. Both Kitchen (*RITA,* 113) and Desroches Noblecourt (*Ramsès II,* 97) suggest that Ramesses became king at the age of twenty-five.

17. This phrase is used on several monuments from Luxor Temple to describe the king at the culmination of the Festival of the Sanctuary.

18. For the key dates in Ramesses II's first few months as king, see Kitchen *RITA,* 191–192. Abydos, Great Dedicatory Inscription.

19. Abydos, Great Dedicatory Inscription.

20. All three quotations are from the Kubban stela. Ramesses' activities in Nubia early in his reign also underline the importance of gold to Egypt's economy; without gold supplies, a king could not finance other royal projects.

21. See Bietak, *Avaris.*

22. Kitchen, *RITA,* 168–172.

23. Quoted in Kitchen, *Pharaoh Triumphant,* 119.

24. Pusch, "Towards a Map of Piramesse"; Pusch, "Piramesse"; Pusch and Herold, "Qantir/Pi-Ramesse."

25. Quoted in Menu, *Ramesses the Great,* 77.

26. Uphill, *The Temples of Per Ramesses.*

27. Quoted in Kitchen, *Pharaoh Triumphant,* 122.

28. Kitchen, *RITA,* 305–312.

CHAPTER 2. WAR AND PEACE

1. Cline, "Hittites."

2. Translation after Güterbock, *The Deeds of Suppiluliuma*, 94–95.

3. Luxor Temple, Moabite campaign inscription; see Darnell and Jasnow, "On the Moabite inscriptions."

4. Kitchen, *RITA*, 1–2.

5. The Battle of Kadesh, "The Poem." The list of Hittite allies provides a veritable gazetteer of kingdoms, vassal states, and loose tribal groupings adjoining the Hittite heartland of central Anatolia. Naharin is the ancient Egyptian term for the Kingdom of Mittani, occupying the great west bend of the Euphrates. Arzawa was a kingdom in southern Anatolia, Dardanaya (Greek Dardanoi, present-day Dardanelles) a territory in western Anatolia. The Keshkesh (or Gasgas) were a group living on the Black Sea coast of northern Anatolia, and the Masa (perhaps Greek Mysia) were another living probably in northwestern Anatolia. Pidasa was a territory in south-central Anatolia, and Irun/Arwanna in an unknown Anatolian location, perhaps adjacent to the lands of the Keshkesh. Karkisha lay in western Anatolia, Lukka (Greek Lycia) in coastal southwest Anatolia, and Kizzuwadna (Greek Cilicia) in southeastern Anatolia. Carchemish is modern Jerablus, on the west bank of the Euphrates; Ugarit, modern Ras Shamra, was an important ancient seaport on the north Syrian coast. Kedy (or Qode) is a generic term for northern Syria; Nuges (or Nuhasse) was a north Syrian kingdom between Aleppo and Hamath, east of the Orontes; Mushanet (or Mushnatu) has been identified with present-day Tell Maraq in Syria.

6. The Battle of Kadesh, "The Poem."

7. Valbelle and Leclère, "Tell Abyad."

8. The Battle of Kadesh, "The Bulletin."

9. The Battle of Kadesh, "The Poem."

10. The Battle of Kadesh, "The Poem."

11. The Battle of Kadesh, "The Poem." For a detailed analysis of the battle, see Kitchen, *RITA*, 8–49; Goedicke, *Perspectives;* Murnane, "Battle of Kadesh."

12. Stela from Giza, near the Great Sphinx, Year 1.

13. The Battle of Kadesh, "The Bulletin."

14. The Battle of Kadesh, "The Poem." Further examples of such similes are found at Abu Simbel (twin stelae in the north and south recesses of the Great Temple), where Ramesses is likened to "a bull with sharp horns," a "victorious lion with tearing claws and resounding roar," a "fire that has caught hold in brushwood, with a gale behind it," and a "storm of resounding thunder out at sea, with mountainous waves."

15. See Habachi, "The Military Posts."

16. Snape, "Ramesses II's Forgotten Frontier," 23.

17. See Snape, "Ramesses II's Forgotten Frontier"; Snape, "Walls, Wells and Wandering Merchants."

18. Van Dijk, "The Canaanite God Hauron."

19. Ramesseum and Luxor Temple inscriptions.

20. See Taraqji, "Nouvelles découvertes"; Yoyotte, "La stèle de Ramsès II"; Kitchen, "Notes on a Stela."

21. See Wimmer, "A New Stela of Ramesses II."

22. Letter from Muwatalli II to Adadnirari I from Boghazkoy, translation after Kitchen, *Pharaoh Triumphant*, 63.

23. See Edel, *Der Vertrag;* Kitchen, *RITA,* 136–145.

24. Peace treaty with the Hittites (Egyptian version).

25. See Edel, *Die ägyptisch-hethitische Korrespondenz.*

26. Letter from Nefertari to Puduhepa, translation after Kitchen, *Pharaoh Triumphant*, 80.

27. Letter from Ramesses II to Hattusili, translation after Kitchen, *Pharaoh Triumphant*, 92.

28. It has been suggested that the Hittite soldiers based at Per-Ramesses may have served as a bodyguard for Ramesses' two Hittite wives (see below, Chapter 4).

CHAPTER 3. A NEW COLOSSUS

1. See Vandersleyen, *L'Égypte et la Vallée du Nil*, 516.

2. Golvin, "Karnak, Temple of Amen-Re."

3. See Yurco, "Representational Evidence."

4. See Murnane, "Luxor, Temple of."

5. Inscription from the sanctuary of Mut, Triple Shrine, Luxor Temple.

6. See Redford, "The Earliest Years of Ramesses II"; Spalinger, "Ramesses II at Luxor."

7. Luxor Temple dedication inscription.

8. Manshiyet el-Sadr stela.

9. See Kitchen, *RITA,* 415–418.

10. See Yurco, "Thebes, the Ramesseum."

11. See Barbotin and Leblanc, *Les monuments.*

12. Kitchen, *RITA,* 442–445.

13. See Rosati, "The Temple of Ramesses II."

14. The circumlocution is found in the tomb of Mes, a private tomb at Saqqara dating to the reign of Ramesses II; the same inscription refers obliquely to Akhenaten as "the enemy of Akhetaten."

15. See Ashmawy and Raue, "Matariya 2016."

16. Kitchen, *RITA,* 501–507, regards Ramesses' Nubian temples as counterparts to, and theologically consistent with, the memorial temples erected at sites throughout Egypt (the Ramesseum, Abydos, Memphis, and Heliopolis).

17. See Ricke, Hughes, and Wente, *The Beit el-Wali Temple;* Fletcher-Jones, *Abu Simbel;* Heidorn, "Nubian Towns and Temples."

18. See El-Achirie and Jacquet, *Le Grand Temple;* Desroches Noblecourt and Kuentz, *Le Petit Temple;* Fletcher-Jones, *Abu Simbel;* Heidorn, "Abu Simbel"; Morkot, "Abu Simbel." The quotation is from Abu Simbel, rock stela no. 9.

19. Abu Simbel, Small Temple, inscription on the facade.

20. See Habachi, *Features of the Deification;* Kitchen, *RITA,* 478–493.

21. Säve-Söderbergh, *Temples and Tombs of Ancient Nubia,* 234.

22. Manshiyet el-Sadr stela; see also Kitchen, *RITA,* 216–217.

23. See Goelet, "The Blessing of Ptah."

24. The "Blessing of Ptah."

25. See Jeffreys, "Memphis."

26. An even larger statue, represented by a solitary fist in the British Museum, would have stood seventy feet tall. Half that size, but still weighing in at 83 tonnes (91.5 tons), is the granite statue, rebuilt from six fragments, that for half a century stood outside the main railway station in Cairo. In August 2006, after half a century looming over Ramesses Square, the statue was relocated to the Grand Egyptian Museum at Giza, to save it from the pollution of the city center.

27. Eaton-Krauss, in "Ramesses-Re Who Creates the Gods," interprets such statues as equating Ramesses with Ra, the creator who called all the other gods into being.

28. The "Blessing of Ptah."

29. Kubban stela.

30. See Kitchen, "Towards a Reconstruction of Ramesside Memphis"; Kitchen, *RITA,* 341–350.

31. See Bárta et al., "The Temple of Ramesses."

32. See Strudwick and Strudwick, *Thebes in Egypt;* Kampp-Seyfried, "Thebes, Dra' Abu el-Naga"; Kampp-Seyfried, "Thebes, el-Asasif"; Kampp-Seyfried, "Thebes, el-Khokha"; Kampp-Seyfried, "Thebes, Sheikh Abd el-Qurna." The change in custom is underlined by a dramatic reduction in the number of private tombs built in the Theban necropolis: from around 350 in the eighteenth dynasty to a mere 80 in the nineteenth dynasty.

33. See Martin, *The Hidden Tombs of Memphis;* Schneider, "Saqqara, New Kingdom Private Tombs."

34. See Martin, *The Tomb of Tia and Tia.*

35. See Daoud, "The Tomb of the Royal Envoy"; Daoud, Farag, and Eyre, "Nakht-Min."

36. Setau, Stela VII, Cairo J.41395.

CHAPTER 4. SONS AND LOVERS

1. Abydos, Great Dedicatory Inscription.

2. Kitchen, *RITA,* 558.

3. Abu Simbel, Small Temple inscription. For the celebration of other female members of the royal family at Abu Simbel, see Desroches Noblecourt, "Abou Simbel."

4. Leblanc, "Isis-Nofret." Two pieces of evidence have been adduced to support this theory: first, Ramesses II chose the rock-cut shrine of Horemheb at Gebel el-Silsila as the place to commemorate his offspring by Isetnofret; second, a relief of Isetnofret was found in Horemheb's Memphite tomb, which was a place of pilgrimage during Ramesses' reign.

5. Statue, Brussels E.7500.

6. See Leblanc, "Henout-Tawy."

7. See Edel, *Die ägyptisch-hethitische Korrespondenz.*

8. See Kitchen, *RITA,* 146–159.

9. Letter of Puduhepa to Ramesses II; translation after Kitchen, *Pharaoh Triumphant,* 84.

10. Letter of Ramesses II to Puduhepa, quoted in Kitchen, *Pharaoh Triumphant,* 85.

11. First Hittite Marriage inscription.

12. Peace treaty with the Hittites.

13. Second Hittite Marriage inscription.

14. Translation after Kitchen, *Pharaoh Triumphant*, 110. On the site and the palace of the royal women at Gurob, see Gorzo, "Gurob."

15. On the daughters, see Dodson and Hilton, *The Complete Royal Families*, 158–175; Sourouzian, "Henout-mi-Rê." Meritamun, statue inscription, quoted in Tyldesley, *Ramesses*, 150.

16. Luxor Temple, Moabite campaign inscription; see Darnell and Jasnow, "On the Moabite Inscriptions."

17. The alternative explanation, that Sethhirkhepeshef was a different son entirely who was promoted to the position of crown prince over the heads of several older brothers, seems highly unlikely.

18. Gomaà, *Chaemwese;* Gomaà, "Khaemwaset."

19. Graffito, Year 23, in a chapel of the pyramid of Khendjer; graffito, Year 47, from the Step Pyramid enclosure.

20. Inscription on the Pyramid of Unas.

21. Inscribed statue of Prince Kawab.

22. See Yoshimura and Takamiya, "A Monument of Khaemwaset."

23. See Jones, "Saqqara, Serapeum and Animal Necropolis."

24. Serapeum inscription.

25. See Leblanc, "Thebes, Valley of the Queens"; Reeves and Wilkinson, *The Complete Valley of the Kings.*

26. Leblanc, "Henout-Tawy"; Leblanc, "L'identification de la tombe." For the identification of Henutmira as a daughter (rather than sister) of Ramesses II, see Sourouzian, "Henout-mi-Rê."

27. Letter from Ramose to Nebnefer and Qaha, translation after Kitchen, *Pharaoh Triumphant,* 125.

28. See Weeks, "Thebes, Valley of the Kings, Tomb KV 5." Documents from Deir el-Medina and the Valley of the Kings suggest that construction of KV5 took place over two decades, between years 20 and 40 of Ramesses II's reign; the Serapeum was built some time after year 30.

29. See Kitchen, *RITA,* 232, 451.

30. Turin Strike Papyrus, quoted in Reeves and Wilkinson, *The Complete Valley of the Kings,* 46.

CHAPTER 5. FROM HERE TO ETERNITY

1. See Barbotin and Leblanc, *Les monuments*, 50. In fact, excavation may have begun even earlier, since the decoration of the first corridor bears signs of having been started before the end of Ramesses' first regnal year (Kitchen, *RITA*, 450).

2. See Leblanc, "The Tomb of Ramesses II," 13.

3. The Bithiah of the Bible (1 Chronicles 4:18), identified as a daughter or granddaughter of Pharaoh, may perhaps have been Bintanat, the daughter or granddaughter of Ramesses III: see Steiner, "Bittĕ-Yâ."

4. See Peden, *The Reign of Ramesses IV*, 93.

5. See Edgerton, "The Strike."

6. Pasebakhaenniut I of the twenty-first dynasty, for example, was buried with an heirloom from the reign of Ramesses II, a ritual brazier.

7. See Vandersleyen, *L'Égypte et la Vallée du Nil*, 556.

8. Genesis 47:11 (Jewish Publication Society, *Tanakh*, 1917); the other Old Testament references to Rameses are Exodus 1:11 and 12:37, and Numbers 33:3.

9. Kitchen, *RITA*, 168, suggests that "Bakhtan" is a misreading of the Egyptian term *Ta-Kheta*, "Land of the Hittites."

10. See Tait, "Setna Khaemwase Cycle."

11. Diodorus Siculus, *The Library of History*, 1.49.6.

12. See Garnett, *The Colossal Statue*.

13. Belzoni, *Narrative of the Operations*, 21.

14. Belzoni, *Narrative of the Operations*, 26.

15. Diodorus Siculus, *The Library of History*, 1.47.4.

16. "Narrative of an Expedition to Explore the River Zaire, Usually Called the Congo, in South Africa, in 1816, Under the Direction of Captain J. H. Tuckey, R.N.; To Which Are Added the Journal of Professor Smith, Some General Observations on the Country and Its Inhabitants; and an Appendix, Containing the Natural History of That Part of the Kingdom of Congo Through Which the Zaire Flows," *Quarterly Review* 18 (1817–1818): 335 ff. (368).

17. Joseph Banks to Henry Salt, February 14, 1819, in Halls, *The Life and Correspondence*, 2:303.

18. Henry Light, "Travels in Egypt, Nubia, Holy Land, Mount Libanon, and Cyprus, in the Year 1814," *Quarterly Review* 19 (April 1818): 178–204 (204).

19. Noeden, "Über das sogennante Memnons-Bild."

20. Belzoni, *Narrative of the Operations,* 80.

21. Christophe, in "Qui, le premier, entra dans le grand temple," has suggested that the first person to enter the temple was not Belzoni himself but his Italian dragoman, Giovanni Finati.

22. Griffith, "The Decipherment of the Hieroglyphs."

23. Henniker, *Notes During a Visit,* 161.

24. Edwards, *A Thousand Miles,* 236–237.

25. Edwards, *A Thousand Miles,* 276–277, 258, 260.

26. Both quotations are taken from an English translation of Maspero's account, published in the *New Zealand Tablet* 18, no. 18 (August 27, 1886): 19.

27. Balout and Roubet, *La momie;* Desroches Noblecourt, *Ramsès II,* 45–57.

28. Edwards, *A Thousand Miles,* 259.

29. Ramesses continued to attract controversy even after the autopsy on his body had been completed. It was reported that fine fragments of tobacco had been found clinging to the mummy (Desroches Noblecourt, *Ramsès II,* 50), prompting wild speculation about possible ancient connections between Egypt and the Americas, and the narcotic habits of the pharaohs. A recent study has concluded, rather more prosaically, that the tobacco probably derived from a nineteenth-century attempt at conservation, using an insecticide containing nicotine (Buckland and Panagiotakopulu, "Ramesses II and the Tobacco Beetle").

30. Quoted in Edwards, *A Thousand Miles,* 282–283.

31. Hayes, *The Scepter of Egypt,* 2:334.

32. Kitchen, *Pharaoh Triumphant,* 235.

33. Edwards, *A Thousand Miles,* 269–270.

34. Jacq, *Ramses: The Son of the Light; Ramses, The Temple of a Million Years; Ramses, The Battle of Kadesh; Ramses, The Lady of Abu Simbel; Ramses, Under the Western Acacia.*

35. See Säve-Söderbergh, *Temples and Tombs.* The operation was a modern feat of engineering to equal the achievements of Ramesses' builders: the artificial hills into which the temples were repositioned have a volume of 11.6 million cubic feet, while the dome above the Great Temple used some 282,000 cubic feet of concrete.

36. Veronese, "A Message from the Director-General."

37. "Abu Simbel: Addresses Delivered at the Ceremony," 27, 29.

38. "Abu Simbel: Addresses Delivered at the Ceremony," 35, 36.

39. "Abu Simbel: Addresses Delivered at the Ceremony," 37.

40. "Abu Simbel: The Campaign."

41. The stela at al-Kiswah may have been set up to mark the renewal of the peace treaty when Tudhalia IV succeeded Hattusili III as Hittite ruler. As Ramesses intended, the treaty continued to be respected by subsequent generations: his successor, Merenptah, sent a shipment of grain to the Hittites to alleviate famine.

42. Edwards, *A Thousand Miles*, 283.

43. For Ramesses' work at Herakleopolis, see Mokhtar, "Relations"; for Buto, see von der Way, "Buto."

Bibliography

Abbas, Mohamed Raafat. "The Bodyguard of Ramesses II and the Battle of Kadesh." *ENiM (Égypte Nilotique et Méditerranéenne)* 9 (2016): 113–123.

"Abu Simbel: Addresses Delivered at the Ceremony to Mark the Completion of the Operations for Saving the Two Temples, Abu Simbel, 22 September 1968." UNESCO, available at https://unesdoc.unesco.org/ark:/48223/pf0000132668 .page=29 (accessed June 15, 2022).

"Abu Simbel: The Campaign That Revolutionized the International Approach to Safeguarding Heritage." UNESCO, available at http://en.unesco.org/70years /abu_simbel_safeguarding_heritage (accessed June 15, 2022).

Allen, James P. "Ramesses I." In *The Oxford Encyclopedia of Ancient Egypt*, ed. Donald B. Redford, 3:116. New York: Oxford University Press, 2000.

Ashmawy, Aiman, and Dietrich Raue. "Matariya 2016: Ramesside Dynasties at Heliopolis." *Egyptian Archaeology* 50 (2017): 16–21.

Balout, Lionel, and C. Roubert. *La momie de Ramsès II*. Paris: Éditions Recherche sur les Civilisations, 1985.

Barbotin, Christophe, and Christian Leblanc. *Les monuments d'éternité de Ramsès II: Nouvelles fouilles thébaines*. Paris: Réunion des Musées Nationaux, 1999.

Bárta, Miroslav, Ladislav Varadzin, Jiří Janák, Jana Mynářová, and Vladimir Brůna. "The Temple of Ramesses II in Abusir." *Egyptian Archaeology* 52 (2018): 10–14.

Belzoni, Giovanni Battista. *Narrative of the Operations and Recent Discoveries Within the Pyramids, Temples, Tombs, and Excavations, in Egypt and Nubia, and of a Journey to the Coast of the Red Sea, in Search of the Ancient Berenice and Another to the Oasis of Jupiter Ammon*. 2nd ed. London: John Murray, 1821.

Bietak, Manfred. *Avaris: The Capital of the Hyksos. Recent Excavations at Tell el-Dab'a*. London: British Museum Press, 1996.

Buckland, P. C., and E. Panagiotakopulu. "Rameses II and the Tobacco Beetle." *Antiquity* 75 (2001): 549–556.

Christophe, Louis-A. "Qui, le premier, entra dans le grand temple d'Abou Simbel." *Bulletin de l'Institut d'Égypte* 47 (1969): 37–45.

Cline, Eric H. "Hittites." In *The Oxford Encyclopedia of Ancient Egypt*, ed. Donald B. Redford, 2:111–114. New York: Oxford University Press, 2000.

Bibliography

Daoud, Khaled. "The Tomb of the Royal Envoy Nakht-Min." *Egyptian Archaeology* 38 (2011): 7–9.

Daoud, Khaled, Sabry Farag, and Christopher Eyre. "Nakht-Min: Ramesses II's Charioteer and Envoy." *Egyptian Archaeology* 48 (2016): 9–13.

Darnell, John Coleman, and Richard Jasnow. "On the Moabite Inscriptions of Ramesses II at Luxor Temple." *Journal of Near Eastern Studies* 52 (1993): 263–274.

Desroches Noblecourt, Christiane. "Abou Simbel, Ramsès, et les dames de la couronne." In *Fragments of a Shattered Visage: The Proceedings of the International Symposium on Ramesses the Great*, ed. Edward Bleiberg and Rita Freed, 127–166. Memphis: Memphis State University, 1991.

——. *Ramsès II: La véritable histoire*. Paris: Pygmalion, 1996.

Desroches Noblecourt, Christiane, and C. Kuentz. *Le Petit Temple d'Abou Simbel: "Nofretari pour qui se lève le Dieu-Soleil,"* 2 vols. Cairo: Centre de documentation et d'étude sur l'ancienne Égypte, 1968.

Dijk, Jacobus van. "The Amarna Period and the Later New Kingdom (c. 1352–1069 BC)." In *The Oxford History of Ancient Egypt*, ed. Ian Shaw, 265–307 ("Rameses II," 288–294). Oxford: Oxford University Press, 2000.

——. "The Canaanite God Hauron and His Cult in Egypt." *Göttinger Miszellen* 107 (1989): 59–68.

Diodorus Siculus. *The Library of History*. Vol. 1: *Books 1–2.34*. Trans. C. H. Oldfather. Loeb Classical Library 279. Cambridge: Harvard University Press, 1933.

Dodson, Aidan, and Dyan Hilton. *The Complete Royal Families of Ancient Egypt*. London: Thames and Hudson, 2004.

Eaton-Krauss, M. "Ramesses-Re Who Creates the Gods." In *Fragments of a Shattered Visage: The Proceedings of the International Symposium on Ramesses the Great*, ed. Edward Bleiberg and Rita Freed, 15–23. Memphis: Memphis State University, 1991.

Edel, Elmar, ed. *Die ägyptische-hethitische Korrespondenz aus Boghazkoi in bablyonischer und hethitischer Sprache*. 2 vols. Opladen: Westdeutscher Verlag, 1994.

——. *Der Vertrag zwischen Ramses II. von Ägypten und Ḫattušili III. von Ḫatti*. Berlin: Gebr. Mann Verlag, 1997.

Edgerton, W. F. "The Strike in Ramesses III's Twenty-Ninth Year." *Journal of Near Eastern Studies* 10 (1951): 137–145.

Edwards, Amelia. *A Thousand Miles up the Nile*. 2nd ed. London: Routledge, 1889.

El-Achirie, H., and J. Jacquet. *Le grand temple d'Abou-Simbel*. Cairo: Centre de documentation et d'étude sur l'ancienne Égypte, 1984.

Bibliography

Fletcher-Jones, Nigel. *Abu Simbel and the Nubian Temples*. Cairo: American University in Cairo Press, 2020.

Freed, Rita E. "Akhenaten's Artistic Legacy." In *Pharaohs of the Sun: Akhenaten, Nefertiti, Tutankhamun*, ed. Rita E. Freed, Yvonne J. Markowitz, and Sue H. D'Auria, 187–197. London: Thames and Hudson, 1999.

Frood, Elizabeth. *Biographical Texts from Ramessid Egypt*. Leiden: Brill, 2007.

Gaballa, Gaballa Ali, and Kenneth A. Kitchen. "Ramesside Varia I." *Chronique d'Égypte* 43 (1968): 259–270.

Garnett, Anna. *The Colossal Statue of Ramesses II*. London: British Museum Press, 2015.

Goedicke, Hans, ed. *Perspectives on the Battle of Kadesh*. Baltimore: Halgo, 1985.

Goelet, Ogden. "The Blessing of Ptah." In *Fragments of a Shattered Visage: The Proceedings of the International Symposium on Ramesses the Great*, ed. Edward Bleiberg and Rita Freed, 28–37. Memphis: Memphis State University, 1991.

Golvin, Jean-Claude. "Karnak, Temple of Amen-Re." In *Encyclopedia of the Archaeology of Ancient Egypt*, ed. Kathryn A. Bard, 400–404. London: Routledge, 1999.

Gomaà, Farouk. *Chaemwese: Sohn Ramses' II. und Hoherpriester von Memphis*. Wiesbaden: Harrassowitz, 1973.

——. "Khaemwaset." In *The Oxford Encyclopedia of Ancient Egypt*, ed. Donald B. Redford, 2:228–229. New York: Oxford University Press, 2000.

Gorzo, Darlene. "Gurob." In *Encyclopedia of the Archaeology of Ancient Egypt*, ed. Kathryn A. Bard, 358–362. London: Routledge, 1999.

Griffith, Frances Llewellyn. "The Decipherment of the Hieroglyphs." *Journal of Egyptian Archaeology* 37 (1951): 38–46.

Güterbock, Hans Gustav. "The Deeds of Suppiluliuma as Told by His Son, Mursili II." *Journal of Cuneiform Studies* 10 (1956): 41–68, 75–98, and 107–130.

Habachi, Labib. *Features of the Deification of Ramesses II*. Glückstadt: J. J. Augustin, 1969.

——. "The Military Posts of Ramesses II on the Coastal Road and the Western Part of the Delta." *Bulletin de l'Institut français d'archéologie orientale* 80 (1980): 13–33.

——. "The Two Rock-Stelae of Sethos I in the Cataract Area Speaking of Huge Statues and Obelisks." *Bulletin de l'Institut français d'archéologie orientale* 73 (1973): 113–125.

Halls, J. J. *The Life and Correspondence of Henry Salt, Esq, F.R.S. &c. His Britannic Majesty's Late Consul-General in Egypt*. 2 vols. London: Richard Bentley, 1834.

Hayes, William C. *The Scepter of Egypt*. 2 vols. Cambridge: Harvard University Press, 1959.

Bibliography

Heidorn, Lisa A. "Abu Simbel." In *Encyclopedia of the Archaeology of Ancient Egypt,* ed. Kathryn A. Bard, 87–90. London: Routledge, 1999.

———. "Nubian Towns and Temples." In *Encyclopedia of the Archaeology of Ancient Egypt,* ed. Kathryn A. Bard, 579–583. London: Routledge, 1999.

Henniker, Sir Frederick, Bt. *Notes During a Visit to Egypt, Nubia, the Oasis, Mount Sinai, and Jerusalem.* London: John Murray, 1823.

Jacq, Christian. *Ramses: The Battle of Kadesh.* Trans. Dorothy S. Blair. London: Simon and Schuster, 1998.

———. *Ramses: The Lady of Abu Simbel.* Trans. Dorothy S. Blair. London: Simon and Schuster, 1998.

———. *Ramses: The Son of the Light.* Trans. Mary Feeney. London: Simon and Schuster, 1997.

———. *Ramses: The Temple of a Million Years.* Trans. Mary Feeney. London: Simon and Schuster, 1997.

———. *Ramses: Under the Western Acacia.* Trans. Mary Feeney. London: Simon and Schuster, 1999.

Jeffreys, David. "Memphis." In *Encyclopedia of the Archaeology of Ancient Egypt,* ed. Kathryn A. Bard, 488–490. London: Routledge, 1999.

———. "Memphis." In *The Oxford Encyclopedia of Ancient Egypt,* ed. Donald B. Redford, 2:373–376. New York: Oxford University Press, 2000.

Jones, Michael. "Saqqara, Serapeum and Animal Necropolis." In *Encyclopedia of the Archaeology of Ancient Egypt,* ed. Kathryn A. Bard, 712–716. London: Routledge, 1999.

Kampp-Seyfried, Friederike. "Thebes, Dra' Abu el-Naga." In *Encyclopedia of the Archaeology of Ancient Egypt,* ed. Kathryn A. Bard, 804–806. London: Routledge, 1999.

———. "Thebes, el-Asasif." In *Encyclopedia of the Archaeology of Ancient Egypt,* ed. Kathryn A. Bard, 802–804. London: Routledge, 1999.

———. "Thebes, el-Khokha." In *Encyclopedia of the Archaeology of Ancient Egypt,* ed. Kathryn A. Bard, 806–807. London: Routledge, 1999.

———. "Thebes, Sheikh Abd el-Qurna." In *Encyclopedia of the Archaeology of Ancient Egypt,* ed. Kathryn A. Bard, 822–824. London: Routledge, 1999.

Kitchen, Kenneth A. "Notes on a Stela of Ramesses II from near Damascus." *Göttinger Miszellen* 173 (1999): 133–138.

———. *Pharaoh Triumphant: The Life and Times of Ramesses II.* Warminster: Aris & Phillips, 1982.

Bibliography

——. "Ramesses II." In *The Oxford Encyclopedia of Ancient Egypt,* ed. Donald B. Redford, 3:116–118. New York: Oxford University Press, 2000.

——. *Ramesside Inscriptions.* 8 vols. Oxford: Blackwell, 1969–1990.

——. *Ramesside Inscriptions Translated and Annotated: Notes and Comments.* Vol. 2: *Ramesses II, Royal Inscriptions.* Oxford: Blackwell, 1999.

——. "Towards a Reconstruction of Ramesside Memphis." In *Fragments of a Shattered Visage: The Proceedings of the International Symposium on Ramesses the Great,* ed. Edward Bleiberg and Rita Freed, 87–104. Memphis: Memphis State University, 1991.

Leblanc, Christian. "Henout-Tawy et la tombe no 73 de la vallée des reines." *Bulletin de l'Institut français d'archéologie orientale* 86 (1986): 203–226.

——. "L'identification de la tombe de Henout-mi-Re fille de Ramsès II et grande épouse royal." *Bulletin de l'Institut français d'archéologie Orientale* 88 (1988): 131–146.

——. "Isis-Nofret, grande épouse de Ramsès II: la reine, sa famille." *Bulletin de l'Institut français d'archéologie Orientale* 93 (1993): 313–333.

——. "Thebes, Valley of the Queens." In *Encyclopedia of the Archaeology of Ancient Egypt,* ed. Kathryn A. Bard, 833–836. London: Routledge, 1999.

——. "The Tomb of Ramesses II and the Remains of His Funerary Treasure." *Egyptian Archaeology* 10 (1997): 11–13.

Martin, Geoffrey T. *The Hidden Tombs of Memphis: New Discoveries from the Time of Tutankhamun and Ramesses the Great.* London: Thames and Hudson, 1991.

——. *The Tomb of Tia and Tia.* London: Egypt Exploration Society, 1997.

Menu, Bernadette. *Ramesses the Great: Warrior and Builder.* London: Thames and Hudson, 1999.

Mokhtar, Gamal. "Relations Between Ihnasya and Memphis During the Ramesside Period." In *Fragments of a Shattered Visage: The Proceedings of the International Symposium on Ramesses the Great,* ed. Edward Bleiberg and Rita Freed, 105–107. Memphis: Memphis State University, 1991.

Morkot, Robert. "Abu Simbel." In *The Oxford Encyclopedia of Ancient Egypt,* ed. Donald B. Redford, 1:4–5. New York: Oxford University Press, 2000.

Murnane, William J. *Ancient Egyptian Coregencies.* Chicago: Oriental Institute, University of Chicago, 1977.

——. "Battle of Kadesh." In *The Oxford Encyclopedia of Ancient Egypt,* ed. Donald B. Redford, 1:166–167. New York: Oxford University Press, 2000.

——. "The Earlier Reign of Ramesses II and His Coregency with Sety I." *Journal of Near Eastern Studies* 34 (1975): 153–190.

Bibliography

——. "Luxor, Temple of." In *Encyclopedia of the Archaeology of Ancient Egypt*, ed. Kathryn A. Bard, 449–453. London: Routledge, 1999.

——. *The Road to Kadesh: A Historical Interpretation of the Battle Reliefs of King Sety I at Karnak*. Chicago: Oriental Institute, University of Chicago, 1985.

Noeden, G. H. "Über das sogenannte Memnons-Bild im Brittischen Museum in London." In George Long, *The British Museum: Egyptian Antiquities*, 1:251. London: Charles Knight, 1832.

Peden, A. J. *The Reign of Ramesses IV.* Warminster: Aris & Phillips, 1984.

Pusch, Edgar B. "Piramesse.'" In *The Oxford Encyclopedia of Ancient Egypt*, ed. Donald B. Redford, 3:48–50. New York: Oxford University Press, 2000.

——. "Towards a Map of Piramesse." *Egyptian Archaeology* 14 (1999): 13–15.

Pusch, Edgar B., and Anja Herold. "Qantir/Pi-Ramesses." In *Encyclopedia of the Archaeology of Ancient Egypt*, ed. Kathryn A. Bard, 647–649. London: Routledge, 1999.

Redford, Donald B. "The Earliest Years of Ramesses II, and the Building of the Ramesside Court at Luxor." *Journal of Egyptian Archaeology* 57 (1971): 110–119.

Reeves, Nicholas, and Richard H. Wilkinson. *The Complete Valley of the Kings*. London: Thames and Hudson, 1996.

Ricke, Herbert, George R. Hughes, and Edward F. Wente. *The Beit el-Wali Temple of Ramesses II*. Chicago: University of Chicago Press, 1967.

Rosati, Gloria. "The Temple of Ramesses II at El-Sheikh Ibada." *Egyptian Archaeology* 28 (2006): 39–41.

Säve-Söderbergh, Torgny, ed. *Temples and Tombs of Ancient Nubia: The International Rescue Campaign at Abu Simbel, Philae and Other Sites*. London: Thames and Hudson/Unesco, 1987.

Schneider, Hans D. "Saqqara, New Kingdom Private Tombs." In *Encyclopedia of the Archaeology of Ancient Egypt*, ed. Kathryn A. Bard, 694–700. London: Routledge, 1999.

Shubert, Steven Blake. "Abydos, Osiris Temple of Seti I." In *Encyclopedia of the Archaeology of Ancient Egypt*, ed. Kathryn A. Bard, 103–104. London: Routledge, 1999.

Smith, Mark. "Gebel el-Silsila." In *Encyclopedia of the Archaeology of Ancient Egypt*, ed. Kathryn A. Bard, 331–334. London: Routledge, 1999.

Snape, Steven. "Ramesses II's Forgotten Frontier." *Egyptian Archaeology* 11 (1997): 23–24.

——. "Walls, Wells and Wandering Merchants: Egyptian Control of Marmarica in the Late Bronze Age." In *Proceedings of the Seventh International Congress of Egyptologists*, ed. C. J. Eyre, 1081–1084. Leuven: Peeters, 1998.

Bibliography

Sourouzian, Hourig. "Ḥenout-mi-Rê, fille de Ramsès II et grande épouse du roi." *Annales du Service des antiquités de l'Égypte* 69 (1983): 365–371.

Spalinger, Anthony. "Ramesses II at Luxor: Mental Gymnastics." *Orientalia* 79 (2010): 425–479.

Steiner, Richard C. "Bittĕ-Yâ, daughter of Pharaoh (1 Chr 4,18), and Bint(i)-'Anat, daughter of Ramesses II." *Biblica* 79 (1998): 394–408.

Strudwick, Nigel, and Helen Strudwick. *Thebes in Egypt: A Guide to the Tombs and Temples of Ancient Luxor.* Ithaca: Cornell University Press, 1999.

Tait, John. "Setna Khaemwase Cycle." In *The Oxford Encyclopedia of Ancient Egypt*, ed. Donald B. Redford, 3:271. New York: Oxford University Press, 2000.

Taraqji, Ahmed Ferzat. "Nouvelles découvertes sur les relations avec l'Égypte à Tel Sakka et à Keswé, dans la région de Damas." *Bulletin de la Société française d'égyptologie* 144 (1999): 27–43.

Tyldesley, Joyce. *Ramesses: Egypt's Greatest Pharaoh.* London: Penguin, 2001.

Uphill, Eric P. *The Temples of Per Ramesses.* Warminster: Aris & Phillips, 1984.

Valbelle, Dominique, and François Leclère. "Tell Abyad: A Royal Ramesside Residence." *Egyptian Archaeology* 32 (2008): 29–32.

Vandersleyen, Claude. *L'Égypte et la Vallée du Nil.* Vol. 2: *De la fin de l'Ancien Empire à la fin du Nouvel Empire.* Paris: Presses Universitaires de France, 1995.

Veronese, Vittorio. "A Message from the Director-General of Unesco." *UNESCO Courier,* February 1960, 3, available at https://unesdoc.unesco.org/ark:/48223/pf0000064522.page=3.

von der Way, Thomas. "Buto (Tell el-Fara'in)." In *Encyclopedia of the Archaeology of Ancient Egypt*, ed. Kathryn A. Bard, 180–184. London: Routledge, 1999.

Weeks, Kent R. "Thebes, Valley of the Kings, Tomb KV 5." In *Encyclopedia of the Archaeology of Ancient Egypt*, ed. Kathryn A. Bard, 831–833. London: Routledge, 1999.

Wegner, Josef W. "Abydos." In *The Oxford Encyclopedia of Ancient Egypt*, ed. Donald B. Redford, 1:7–12. New York: Oxford University Press, 2000.

Wimmer, Stefan Jakob. "A New Stela of Ramesses II in Jordan in the Context of Egyptian Royal Stelae in the Levant." *Third International Congress on the Archaeology of the Ancient Near East (3ICAANE),* Paris, April 18, 2002.

Yoshimura, Sakuji, and Izumi Takamiya. "A Monument of Khaemwaset at Saqqara." *Egyptian Archaeology* 5 (1994): 19–23.

Yoyotte, Jean. "La stèle de Ramsès II à Keswé et sa signification historique." *Bulletin de la Société française d'égyptologie* 144 (1999): 44–58.

Bibliography

Yurco, Frank J. "Representational Evidence, New Kingdom Temples." In *Encyclopedia of the Archaeology of Ancient Egypt,* ed. Kathryn A. Bard, 671–674. London: Routledge, 1999.

——. "Thebes, the Ramesseum." In *Encyclopedia of the Archaeology of Ancient Egypt,* ed. Kathryn A. Bard, 812–814. London: Routledge, 1999.

Index

Index

Index

81–89, 94–98, 109–116; cartouches of, 82; children of, as depicted on royal monuments, 128, 130–131; coming of age of, 31–33; coronation of, 117–118; damage to tomb of, 156; daughters of, 129; death of, 155; as defender of religious orthodoxy, 96–97; as depicted at Abu Simbel, 101–106; as depicted on monuments, 21–22, 24, 38, 53–62, 69–71, 85, 98, 134, 186–187; discovery of mummy of, 174–175; as divine king, 98–107; fallen colossus of, 162–163; family background of, 3–4, 12; as father, 3, 118, 128–134, 185–186; favored queens of, 118–119; in film and literature, 181–182; grave goods of, 154–155; harem of, 118, 128; and Hattusili, 123, 126–127; historians' perspective on, 161; Hittite wives of, 123–128; as honored in temples at Memphis, 110–112; as husband, 118; as joint ruler with his father, 25–26, 117; jubilees (*sed*-festivals) celebrating reign of, 142–143; and legitimacy of his dynasty, 134; memorial temple of, 89–94; military responsibilities of, 17–19; military victories of, 21–22, 185; monuments of, as tourist attraction, 170–171; names associated with, 38; narrative tales relating to, 159–160; ongoing fascination with, 178–188; and peace treaty with Hatti, 74–79; preparations for the afterlife by, 152–153; reputation of, 1–2, 4–5, 158, 185–186; royal apprenticeship of, 18, 20–21; and sense of dynastic destiny, 118; sons of, 129–134; speculations on character of, 179–180; sunk relief as used for monuments

of, 32–33; throne names of, 25–26, 31–32, 104; tomb of, 148–149, 150, 152–156; well ordered by, 31; wives of, 118–119, 122–126. *See also* Abu Simbel; Abydos; Heliopolis; Karnak; Luxor Temple; Memphis; Per-Ramesses; Ramesses' mummy; Ramesseum

Ramesses III (Usermaatra-meryamun), 157

Ramesses IV, 157

Ramesses, Prince (son of Ramesses II), 143; burial place of, 149; as crown prince, 131, 134

Ramesses-Meretmirra, 133

Ramesses-Meryamun, 132

Ramesses-Meryamun-Nebweben, 133

Ramesses-Payotnetjer, 133

Ramesses-Userpehty, 133

Ramesses' mummy: condition of, 176–177; discovery of, 174–175; photo of, 178; return of, to Cairo, 177–178; unwrapping of, 175–176

Ramesseum: abandonment of, 159; as administrative center for Thebes, 157–158; architect of, 91; description of, 91–94; as memorial temple of Ramesses II, 89–94, 145, 187; Ramesses as divine king at, 98; workers' protest at, 158

Ramose, 75

Reshep, 40

Rosetta Stone, 169

Salt, Henry, 163, 164–165, 182

Samontu, 133

Saqqara (necropolis of Memphis), 12, 110

Sartre, Jean-Paul, 183

Satra (wife of Paramessu/Ramesses I), 12, 145

Second Intermediate Period, 34

Index